Coffee, Chianti and Caravaggio

COFFEE, CHIANTI AND CARAVAGGIO

by

❖Robert Noble Graham❖

www.rngnovels.co.uk

copyright 2014 Robert Noble Graham

cover art designed and produced by

Louise Macdonald

Coffee, Chianti and Caravaggio

This book is dedicated especially to my wonderful children Abi and Malcolm but also to the many other people who figure in it who helped to enhance my experiences of a great country

About the Author

Robert Noble Graham had a career in the oil, publishing and finance industries. He is a graduate in French and German and in English. He is divorced with two adult children, both scientists. He has written drama that has been produced on BBC Radio 4 and in Scottish theatres. He has contributed specialist financial articles to various journals and is a regular contributor to Mensa magazine. He lives in Scotland and is the author of travel books and novels:

By The Same Author

Novels

- MASKS OF VENICE
- THE CELEBRITY OF ANDERS HECHT
- THE WOMEN FROM CRETE

Travel Books

- COFFEE IN CUBA
- COFFEE, CASTANETS AND DON QUIXOTE

All of the above are available either as e-books or print books.

CONTENTS:

- INTRODUCTION...6
- THE CHIANTI HILLS -TUSCANY............8
- SKIRTING THE UNDERWORLD , SAILING TO CAPRI FROM SORRENTO..........28
- THE OVERWHELMING CITY -ROME..................51
- THE LAND OF PRINCES AND SECRET WINES - LIGURIA...............69
- THE COMPANY IN VENICE................82
- DIVINE COMEDY IN FLORENCE...........96
- BANQUET IN BOLOGNA...........116

Coffee, Chianti and Caravaggio

Introduction

I have often been struck by the extent to which some relatively small areas of the planet have profoundly affected history whilst some vast tracts have made no apparent impact at all. I gather that advanced mathematical theories can show that a dung beetle strolling across the Sahara can make Wall Street collapse or a penguin having breakfast in Antarctica can cause bumper crops in India. Maybe plunging needles into voodoo dolls works as well. I don`t know. What is clear to me is that Italy is one of these relatively small areas of land that have left a major impact on millions of lives. The Roman Empire influenced law, language, road-building, religion and thought. Artists like Raphael and Titian, musicians like Verdi and Vivaldi, writers like Dante and Tasso all created universes. Visitors love its food, its climate, its wonderful cities and its landscapes. We follow its fashion and drink its wine. Its sons and daughters have travelled far and wide, sometimes to serve us pizza or ice cream, sometimes to become great entertainers like Frank Sinatra, Tony Bennett, Robert de Niro or Al Pacino. Northern artists and aristocrats considered it an essential part of The Grand Tour. Goethe, Ibsen, Schopenhauer, Stendhal, Wagner, Henry James , Tchaikovsky, Byron, Shelley, Browning and many others were all captivated by it. Many millions of less august visitors pour into it every year, but many are dazzled by its endless variety.

That immense creativity is, of course, not the whole story. The Roman Empire caused widespread bloodshed and brutality. War and crime have been constants through much of its history. Even today the probity of its politics is not universally admired. Some people feel the turmoil and corruption are in some way essential for the accomplishments. Yet there can be few countries that can offer more to delight and interest the visitor than Italy. In so many areas of life it has wonders to offer.

I have now visited Italy quite often and have a working knowledge of the language. I don`t pretend to be an expert in any part of it so this book is about the one area I know better than anyone: my own reactions and experiences on these visits, sometimes accompanied and sometimes alone. Italy has many faces and identities, some of which are constant and some of which change subtly and regularly. There are a lot of clichés about it. I think it`s a good idea to sweep them out of your mind before going. It is bound to surprise you.

THE CHIANTI HILLS -TUSCANY

My first trip to Italy took me to Tuscany. My son, Malcolm, was thirteen. Since his sister had gone off to university there were just the two of us. I had booked accommodation on a Chianti estate in the hills to the east of Florence. The month was July, when Scottish schools, unlike English ones, are on holiday. I had arranged to pick up a car at Pisa airport although I had heard alarming things about Italian driving. However, it was the only way we could reach our accommodation, so it was necessary. Travelling with a youngster can be a great experience. It was a delight to see how entranced Malcolm was by the sight of the Alps below as we flew over them.

I had encouraged myself to view driving on Italian autostradas as a form of chariot racing. If I stayed in the slow lane then the Ferraris and Lamborghinis could re-enact Ben Hur in the fast lane without troubling us. I`m not sure where I picked up this view of Italian traffic dangers. They don`t rank badly amongst European countries for road accidents, which in turn rank well compared to anywhere else. I believe the statistics in Rome are not good. That probably distorts the figure for the whole country. The idea of mad Italian drivers was just another stereotype of which travelling cured me. In fact, I soon began to relax and enjoy the experience.

With that anxiety allayed I began to realize that I was hungry. I suggested to Malcolm that we find a place to eat and his agreement was enthusiastic. We pulled off and stopped in a village in the nearby hills. This gave us our next chance to throw a stereotype in the bin. If we had imagined that Italians ate pasta and pizzas from the dolomites to the south of Sicily we had a sudden re - education. We were introduced to traditional Tuscan cooking with a stew of pork, tomatoes, garlic and beans after a plate of prosciutto. Unexpected but very palatable.

Malcolm proved to be a good navigator and we found our way past Florence on the road to Pontassieve. We thought that an attractive, Italian name but the place was drab and industrial. I hoped it was not an indication of what was ahead of us. This whole area south of Florence is the Chianti. That`s not the name of any grape or wine producer. So, some of the wine bearing that name is well worth drinking and some could more usefully clean the bath. The weather was sunny but not too hot. The country outside of Pontassieve was green with the high hills and rows of cypress trees so typical of the area. We then took the road to Rosano from which a sign directed us 3 km along to the estate. This road was a steep narrow track with a rudimentary sign` Castiglionchio`, our destination. I turned into it and was very glad this was not a cycling holiday. The track was rough and climbed sharply past a dark green grove of olive trees on the right. I began to worry about just what it was I had booked. How primitive could Italy get? I had been attracted by the setting of this place and the idea of being in the hills near Florence on a Chianti estate. However, only as I drove did it trouble me that I had really not given as much thought as I should to how comfortable Malcolm would be? He was simply trusting that I would have organized it perfectly with that confidence in parents that, sadly, is not always well placed.

Eventually, with relief, we rounded a bend and saw a magnificent estate house sitting on the hill. To the left we saw fields with vines. We were in Chianti country. I remember clearly how we parked the car and got out to magnificent hilltop scenery. Looking over the olive grove we had passed were smaller hills surrounding little towns with church towers. Further on we could see the high Appenines over which we would watch the sun set in the warm evenings. All of this was on a sunny day under a blue sky. I think the first impression on both of us was very good.

We went to the main house which has, I gather, subsequently been upgraded into a magnificent set of apartments. Even then it had rooms you could stay in, but we had opted for the converted outbuildings. More rustic, we thought. Cheaper too. Once we had registered we made our way in some excitement and sense of triumph along the path, past a small grove of cypress trees to a grassy area about as wide as a football pitch. It was bounded on the left by a low wall. Beyond it the hill rose steeply past one of the swimming pools to dense woods at the top. We were at an altitude of around 1,000 metres (3,000 feet) and to the right was the view past the dark green olive groves to the little town of Pelago whose rooftops were just visible amongst lower hills. We saw there was a break in the wall on the left. Following instructions, we crossed to it where a well trodden path was visible. Even before we reached it we could see a long stone- built building to the right of the path. It had presumably at one time been stables or haylofts. It sat in a hollow which offered merciful shade from the sun which was now hot. We reached it by going down a short flight of steps leading to a terrace in front of the building. The terrace was neatly laid out with gravel chips and on it stood round white tables with chairs.

There were perhaps eight apartments in this block of outbuildings. Ours was the second last from the top. This meant that our section of the terrace had quite a lot of shade from the hillside that rose sharply above it. This proved to be a very welcome factor since, as we discovered, July in Italy can be like a vacation in a frying pan. With some eagerness we opened the door to see what we had booked. The brochure had not been very detailed on this matter and I worried that it might be all too obviously a converted stable. We entered to see a room with a stone floor. It was spacious with a simple but adequate cooker against one wall. Against the other was a bed under a wooden platform on which was another bed. A wooden staircase led up to the platform. Considering that we hoped to spend most of our week outside this looked like very acceptable accommodation. It was primitive enough to make us feel like manly, Spartan types without offering any serious inconvenience. As we were shortly to discover, it was a little closer to raw nature than we at first thought.

If we went back out of the door and up the steps we were on the steep, very green hillside with two swimming pools a couple of hundred metres back towards the main house and, just uphill a little, a tennis court. Malcolm was a good tennis player who did well in the league back home. I was good enough to give him a worthwhile game so that was a bonus.

Since we had not yet done any shopping we drove down to Pelago for a meal. It is an attractive little town with a large main square. There we found a good restaurant with a friendly waiter. The food was excellent and I decided to get some advice about a prospective trip to Florence which was high on our agenda of places to visit. It was a favourite city of Henry James who situated the later chapters of his great novel *Portrait of a Lady* there. In

Puccini`s opera *Gianni Schicchi* the old rascal`s daughter sings *o mio babbino caro* (Oh my beloved father) in which she says she would go to Porta Rossa to buy a wedding ring and if her love failed she would throw herself from the Ponte Vecchio into the Arno, also in Florence. It was the home of the great Uffizi Gallery and Michelangelo`s statue of David. It was also the ancient home of the Florentine bankers who once financed emperors and popes. It was where Dante Alighieri at the age of 9 first saw and fell in love with Beatrice Portinari, aged 8, which led to the first, and possibly greatest, poem of post classical Europe, *La Divina Commedia.* It had a football team in Serie A which Malcolm often watched on Sundays. The list of attractions and great artistic and historical references goes on. We only had a short time so I needed some guidance on where to begin. At this time I didn`t really speak Italian, but the waiter`s English was good and he was quite extrovert. So, I put my question to him. He thought for a moment and said: "There`s a great Irish pub just off the Via Romana."

By the time we had eaten and taken a short stroll around Pelago it was getting dark. The day had gone well so we drove back up to Castiglionchio, parked the car and walked across the wide grassy stretch that led to the wall, beyond which was our lodging. As we approached the break in the wall we were enchanted by the sight of tiny lights dancing through the air in front of us. Neither of us had ever seen fireflies before and it took us a moment to understand that was what we were witnessing. Apparently they are not flies but beetles of the Luciola genus. Evidently their glow not only attracts members of the opposite sex but, allegedly, helps them to attract suitable mates. This seems a considerable improvement on the dating sites used by humans which are costly and any glow that ensues is usually from embarrassment. Just as we were about to enter our apartment we became aware of a more sinister aspect of the local fauna. From the dense woods high up on the hill we heard the cry of wolves. We had never before heard that sound except in films and it is amazingly eerie. I associated it with Jack London novels set in frozen forests in Canada. I had not known they were still found in the wild in Italy. They used to be native to Scotland and there is a drive to reintroduce them as predators to control the red deer population. Advocates claim their hostile reputation is undeserved, but long before Jack London wolves figured in old English and Scandinavian tales as fearsome enemies. I used to live in a Scottish town named Balfron which derives from the Gaelic *Bal fruin* or "town of sorrows" because at the end of the eighteenth century wolves came down from the Campsie Hills and killed several children. We locked the door securely.

As it happened, we were still not done with the attentions of Italian wild life. We were now quite tired and went to bed. I found the apartment comfortable and peaceful so I slept well and awoke fairly early. I crept downstairs as quietly as possible to make some tea. In fact, Malcolm was already awake but was taking his time about getting up.

"Sleep well?" I asked.

"Yes, once I got used to the noise."

I was surprised since I had thought the place very quiet.

"What noise was that?"

"Woodworm eating my bed."

I laughed, assuming he was joking.

"You`ve been having strange dreams. Must have been the Italian food."

"Come over and listen."

I went over and lay on the bed beside him. We were quiet for a moment and then I too heard the distinct noise of munching. Something indeed was eating Malcolm`s bed. He laughed when he realized I believed him.

"Do you think my bed will last the week?"

Evidently the stables had been converted using untreated wood. I had no idea how long it would take woodworm to digest an entire bed frame but I thought it would probably see us through. If not, then the pile of sawdust would probably be good evidence for a money back claim.

We had no food at this stage so after some tea we set off to a nearby village called Borselli where we bought bread, butter, prosciutto, tomatoes and an excellent cheese called sardo peccorini. We returned and sat outside with our feast which tasted quite delicious. There we met our next door neighbour, Sven, from Sweden. Like most Swedes I've encountered, he spoke good English and he seemed eager to chat. He told us he was there with his wife and daughter but they didn't appear for breakfast. He showed considerable interest in what we were eating and thought it a remarkably bold thing to do to buy local ham and cheese and eat it with local bread. We never quite asked him directly but his conversation implied that every scrap they ate had been brought from Stockholm in cool boxes. Having said that, I don't recall ever seeing him eat anything. Since this was the first day of my first visit to Italy I had little evidence to go on, but the rest of that week and my subsequent visits have fully confirmed our impression at that initial breakfast that Italian food is second to none for variety, freshness, flavour and methods of preparation. I have no direct experience of Swedish cooking but I have never heard it praised to the extent that one should avoid local Italian gastronomy in favour of what you brought from Scandinavia in a cool box.

Robert Noble Graham

After breakfast we strolled around the estate. With the help of a map I realized that to one side we could see Vallombrosa which Milton refers to in *Paradise Lost* in connection with Galileo. It was believed for a long time that Milton had actually visited the site which had a monastery dating from the eleventh century, but he probably was never there. However, many of his admirers such as Wordsworth and Mary Shelley made their way there in the probably mistaken belief they were following in the footsteps of their hero. The Abbey was also, in 1096, the rallying point chosen by Pope Urbino II to launch a crusade to liberate Christianity. To the north was the city of Fiesole, a commercial centre as far back as Etruscan times and known for important works by Fra Angelico. It was also cited later by Robert Browning as the home of Andrea del Sarto, "the flawless painter". Andrea is shown in the poem bearing his name having a strained conversation with his wife Lucrezia. Browning makes it obvious that any charm Lucrezia had found in being the wife of a well-known artist had long since faded. You feel she is regretting not having been born in the 21st century when she could have gone out clubbing of an evening.

  The estate itself was clearly very old. It had apparently been a fortified town at one stage in its history, possibly recalling the fourteenth and fifteenth centuries in Italy when the country was in a kind of phoney war. The different city states were great rivals and their cause was championed by the *condottieri* , bands of soldiers who rode around in splendid pomp with magnificent weaponry but who hardly ever engaged in real combat. They were mercenaries. Getting into serious action would have damaged equipment and therefore undermined profits. Instead, they became masters of the threatening gesture and the intimidating livery. I should think Castiglionchio would have been quite easily defended. It would not have been large or rich enough to attract serious attention and it would only have been with extreme reluctance that any horse would have agreed to climb the steep hillside with a heavily armed man on his back, regardless how much of a parody he was of a real soldier. The pantomime nature of the condottieri world was illustrated by the Battle of Zagonara in 1424 which went on for hours and hardly a drop of blood was spilt. Having said that, they did defend the Italian states effectively against several foreign incursions. However, they couldn`t withstand the savage attacks launched by the French king, Charles VIII, to try to distract his citizens from the murderous religious wars raging in France itself during the Hundred Years war. Part of the reason for that was in the nature of the condottieri. They were mercenaries and felt no need to fight for their country if there were more money helping the enemy. I`m not very proud to say that the French were also assisted by companies of Scottish archers, allegedly gigantic and terrifying. The French, by then ruled by Francis I were eventually defeated and repelled at the Battle of Pavia in 1524. The turning point was the entry to the fray of the Habsburg emperor, Charles V with an army of 20,000. The French were entirely routed and Francis was imprisoned in Madrid. This was because Charles was Spanish and that part of northern Italy then had to be content with Spanish rule rather than French. It is said that many of the Scots, unable to get back home, settled in Italy in a town called Gurro where the dialect evidently shows marked Scottish traits to this day.

Malcolm and I continued our exploration by walking along the rough path that led back to the Rosano road . It was also steep but the view from it down to the little village of Pelago was lovely. The highway was quiet, but suddenly we discovered to our alarm the true danger of Tuscan thoroughfares. I had become quite relaxed about Italian traffic, but had not given much thought to the murderous nature of bicycles. I have in my time been a little irritated by the imperious hordes of cyclists on occasions in the Netherlands and by the students in Cambridge who don`t bother with lights at night as they whizz along, no doubt certain that their mighty intellects glow for all to see. However, I had never previously considered them life-threatening. Suddenly as we took our leisure on this quiet but very steep road I heard a faint "zip" and yelled to Malcolm to "Look out!!" Fortunately, his instincts saved

Coffee, Chianti and Caravaggio

him as a stick-thin black figure appeared at the top of the hill and rocketed down probably faster than the speed limit for cars. At that velocity he could have sliced through an elephant, but probably the smallest impediment would have been fatal for him.

We strolled back in thoughtful mood which probably explains why we were foolish enough to play tennis in the noonday sun. Along with the intense heat we often could not see the ball if it was above shoulder height because of the blinding sun. In no time I had a headache. Malcolm was annoyed with himself for playing badly, and we decided to have lunch. Our shaded terrace was a blessing. We put together a very reasonable pasta dish with fresh basil and parmesan cheese and went out to our table on the terrace. Sven was already sitting there and he greeted us. We told him how foolish we had been trying to play tennis. He was sympathetic and said that his daughter played and would probably enjoy a light-hearted match with Malcolm. We welcomed that idea but had still seen no sign of this daughter or indeed of his wife who was, apparently, also on holiday with him. Nor had we ever seen him eat or drink anything. Although it was lunchtime we saw no evidence that he had taken any nourishment or intended to do so.

Since we had a car and my regard for Italian driving had risen we decided to explore. We set out for the city of

Robert Noble Graham

Arezzo. We knew very little about it other than that it could be reached easily from our lodgings. We set off on route 70 which would take us directly to the city. The weather was good and the countryside attractive. Other than bursts of anxiety when cyclists whirled into view we were tranquil as we discussed the probable outcome of the rugby world cup which was taking place at the time in South Africa. It seemed inevitable that the mighty All Blacks from New Zealand would sweep the tournament, not least because of the presence of the extraordinary Jonah Lomu in the team. At 6 feet 5 ins tall and 125 kilograms in weight he also had remarkable speed. His ability to outrun small rugby players and steam-roller large ones at times seemed to make team mates superfluous.

At mid morning we reached the small but ancient town of Bibbiena where a fine outdoor café had been considerately sited overlooking a spectacular gorge. We sat under the shade of a parasol and admired the impressive scene. A slim waiter with stylishly trimmed hair and a languid gait strode up to us as if no job on earth could be as enviable as that of an Italian waiter in Bibbiena. Malcolm photographed the gorge and the café . The setting was perfect for our coffee break. The day was becoming warmer and already we were feeling some of the temptation to idle longer than necessary. However, we had our aims for the day. We paid and left.

The trip to Arezzo really demonstrated great faith in the beauty and variety of Italy. There are not many countries where I would have devoted one day of a short holiday to an outing without research. At times it crossed my mind that we might regret the adventure, but in fact a great spectacle was in store for us. We reached the city and parked just outside the walls of the ancient part. From there we walked up through the old stone gates on a quiet road which was clearly hundreds of years old. This led to the magnificent Piazza Grande dating from 1573. It had a mixture of buildings. Some had the familiar ochre walls with red roofs. Others were taller with dark stone and crenellated tops. On one side is the arcade, a fine series of arches designed by Giorgio Vasari. Vasari was a native of the town although his gifts and contacts took him far and wide. You can visit his house in which, I gather, he painted an allegory of vice and virtue. Evidently it has the characteristic that as you walk around the house sometimes one seems to be winning and sometimes the other. He knew life. The old centre had been very badly damaged in the Second World War but much of it remains. The city has had much to put up with since it has been an important settlement from Etruscan times on. In early times it carried on civilized trade and cultural exchange with Greece as many artefacts attest. Then the Romans came along under Sulla and, in line with their particular view of spreading civilization they demolished half of the city. Romans of that time were very good soldiers, engineers and administrators, but they didn`t really do sensitivity. I remember watching a BBC TV programme when I was very young in which a panel of experts were asked to identify antiques and remains. The famous archaeologist Sir Mortimer Wheeler was shown a vase. He turned it over in his hands with a long-suffering expression and said "Bad enough to be Roman" which indeed it was. They were not alone in this of course. Long after their decline Arezzo was one of many parts of Italy invaded by Germanic tribes. The name "Lombardy" is in fact derived from the "Langobardi" a Germanic tribe who apparently had not discovered the joys of shaving since the name means `the long-bearded ones`. They knew how to demolish a good palace however. The appalling destructive power of the Second World War gave evidence of just how far Europeans have progressed since these early, untutored days when the best thing the Aretines could do was welcome Greek merchants with excellent food and wine and trade delicate kitchenware.

Mercifully, one treasure that has survived destructive attention is the great fresco cycles of Piero della Francesca, *The Legend of the True Cross.* Piero was also a native of the city and many of his works can be found in it as can some by other artists such as Cimabue. Arezzo has also succeeded in becoming quite wealthy, mainly as a result of farming and a thriving jewellery industry.

We walked towards the very large cathedral to the north of the square when suddenly we heard what sounded like horses galloping. To our astonishment round the corner of the duomo came a group of mediaeval knights. Both riders and horses were decked in ornate yellow and blue livery as if for jousting. What was happening? Had we stumbled onto a film set? In no time another group appeared, similarly decked out except that the colour was red and green. A blue and yellow group followed and finally a yellow and crimson one arrived. Crowds of the townsfolk came after them. It was obviously a festival, but of what we could not guess until later we discovered that we had happened upon the famous *Giostra dei Saraceni* or Joust of the Saracens, played out every year at this time. It becomes a very elaborate display and has existed on and off since the 14th century with one district of the city competing with the others at a jousting competition where a dummy is the target. We watched this for a time, dazzled. There came a lull in the action eventually and we assumed the event was tailing off. It was time for lunch anyway so we went away from the square, took some more photographs and decided to head back after eating. We had to do some shopping for the evening meal and, since we had spent so much time in the car, we thought we should get some exercise. It was only later that we discovered the Joust of the Saracens went on for most of the day. I doubt if we would have watched much more of it anyway since we didn't really understand what it was all about, but the spectacle had thrilled us.

We were already impressed by the friendliness and humour of the Italian people. My subsequent visits to Italy have confirmed that impression with the exception of the first visit I made to Venice when everyone seemed grumpy. I put that down to a surfeit of tourists. I was delighted my young son was having that experience. He already had a favourable view of the Spanish from early contacts we had. I felt such encounters would be good insulation against the xenophobia that all peoples exhibit at times and certain of our daily papers resort to regularly when sales are poor.

We arrived back in the late afternoon and, inspired by the exploits of Jonah Lomu, we decided to play with Malcolm's rugby ball for a time. The grassy area downhill from the converted outbuildings where we were lodging was wide enough to be able to throw and kick in safety. It was good exercise after a day in the car. As we finished so I could begin cooking we noticed Sven standing watching us. "What happened to your ball?" he asked.

We didn't understand.

"It's out of shape."

We recalled that Sweden, always impressive in soccer, was not known for its rugby players.

"It's a rugby ball," we advised. Sven's face suggested inner turmoil. What is it about that phrase, he clearly wondered, that justified playing with a ball that was clearly out of shape? He probably consoled himself with the thought that the English (as he no doubt considered us) are notably eccentric. He decided to move to common ground. He looked at Malcolm.

"Shall I ask my daughter if she'd like to play tennis?"

Malcolm answered enthusiastically. The sun was lower in the sky but it was still hot and I was not sorry that he would have another opponent, although I did enjoy playing. He went to get his racquet and Sven to consult the daughter we had not yet seen. I retreated to our mercifully cool apartment and began cooking. After ten minutes Malcolm came back in.

"What's wrong? Is she not ready yet?" I queried.

He shrugged. "She's not playing."

"Why not?"

"Religious reasons."

I struggled with that answer. I thought of the ten commandments, the seven deadly sins, the Beatitudes . "Blessed are they who don't agree to play tennis as the sun goes down," was not an instruction that had caught my attention at any time, but I didn't like to be dogmatic.

Robert Noble Graham

Later Sven, still unaccompanied, explained that his 13 year old daughter was studying for the ministry and felt playing tennis with a boy would not be proper. I longed to advise the young lady that history was full of the murders and atrocities carried out by churches and other religious organizations which did not play much tennis. I had never heard of `the tennis crusades ` or `the purging of the ball boys` or even `the four umpires of the Apocalypse. ` However, it was not my place to unpick the ancient prejudices and fantasies so assiduously acquired.

We next set off for Florence. Other than the hearty recommendation for its Irish pub I had no clear idea which of its many wonders we should seek out first. Malcolm was in no doubt. We should find a newsagent and see who had won the rugby world cup. I thought that a fine plan since I felt it could be linked with my own daily preoccupation of finding a decent café for my taste of forbidden pleasure. So charmed was I by this agenda and so serene had I become about driving in Italy that I came close to causing a nasty accident with a scooter rider. The near –miss haunts me to this day since it would have been entirely my fault. Malcolm, I believe, is still unaware of it.

It was with some relief that I parked in an underground public facility and we came up to the burning hot streets of Florence in early July. Disobeying the instruction of the fine old song, we did not direct our feet to the sunny side of the street. We found shade wherever possible and crept along beside the mercifully tall buildings that cast long shadows. It thrilled me finally to be in this city so intimately involved with the beginning of the Renaissance and with so much creativity. With some excitement we found a vendor selling The Daily Telegraph and headed for one of the many cafés. There we entered a scene that became very familiar to me over the years. Customers, whether male or female, stylishly dressed, stood at the counter arguing and gesticulating loudly and energetically but good-humouredly. We had the strong, rich smell of good coffee and, although the café was busy, we had no trouble finding an empty table, since Italians at that time of day so rarely sit. They knock back their tiny cups of very strong espresso, take some water, debate vigorously and then set off. I left Malcolm at the table to turn the pages. I went to the counter and, feeling very alien and stupid, blundered my way through the strange system of obtaining refreshment. The staff were perfectly friendly and polite but they were geared up to the dynamic executive or the expat who had mastered the system. Eventually I got us some food and some drinks and went back to the table. Malcolm looked up, a little stunned.

"The South Africans won 15-12"

I was surprised. They were the host nation and I wondered if there had been a bit of favouritism.

"Not according to this," explained Malcolm. "Apparently Stransky and van der Westhuizen were great and the Kiwis more or less froze."

Fortunately, we had no money on the result and we didn't really care that much who won. It was simply one of these shocks that sport delivers. Later it emerged that in fact some major controversies had ensued with accusations and counter-accusations but that is history.

We wandered the short distance into the centre and Malcolm used his camera to record the Duomo (the cathedral), the Palazzo Vecchio and the statue of David (now a copy since the decision in 1881 to protect the original by putting it away from the elements in the Accademia.) Malcolm suggested the view from the top of the Duomo would be worth getting. I had some sympathy with the sub-plot that whilst climbing the steps might be an effort it would be cooler than standing in the frying pan of the main square. Despite the heat, however, we did pause to admire the orange- tiled dome that the great Brunelleschi designed for it. To Italian eyes it may not be so remarkable, but British cathedrals just do not look like that, neither in shape nor colour. In fact the climb was well worth it. The view over the red tiled tops with the tower of the Palazzo Vecchio in the near distance and the hills in the background made a great scene. Perhaps it was particularly striking to us since it was so different from any view available in Britain. It was thoroughly Italian and we approved of that.

On coming back out we could not ignore the amazing east doors of the Baptistry, cast in bronze by Lorenzo Ghiberti to give thanks for the city's release from the plague in 1401. Michelangelo termed them "The Gates of Paradise". Ghiberti won this commission in competition with giants such as Donatello and Brunelleschi himself. His design was so radically different from anything seen before that he was a worthy winner.

We walked on past great work by Donatello and Giambologna, past the Uffizi gallery itself. I have been asked "how could you go to Florence and not visit the Uffizi? " Well, I could use Malcolm as an excuse and explain that it would be unkind to drag a 13 year old boy who had not been granted his wish of visiting a football match through such an adult experience. In truth I couldn't face it myself. For the first time in Italy but by no means for the last I was simply overwhelmed by the treasures that are simply part of the fabric of the city. I suggested we head for the river and buy an ice cream.

Malcolm approved of this idea but I did not have the impression he was bored. Frequent visits to great locations have convinced me you do not have to visit the famous sites to be energized by their vitality. We were both having a wonderful day without trying to do more than nibble at the great banquet that is a major Italian city.

We reached the Arno, bought our ice cream and went to see the Ponte Vecchio. According to H.V. Morton this famous old bridge used to house many of the city`s butchers. However, when in 1565 Cosimo I, Duke of Tuscany, moved his residence across the river he felt he did not want to look out at the meat markets. That`s when the decision was taken to replace the butchers with jewellers, felt to be more in keeping with Cosimo`s sensibilities, and that`s where they still are. As we enjoyed our ice creams in some merciful shade by the river I, rather pompously, explained the story of the 9 year old Dante falling in love with the 8 year old Beatrice. He never saw her again and on her death while the great poet was in exile from his native Tuscany he began the unique poem which was one of the first great landmarks of the Renaissance in Europe, with Florence often cited as its cradle. I explained that this immense rebirth of culture then moved northward. I got what I deserved when Malcolm asked me why the Renaissance had begun in Florence. I couldn`t answer it then and perhaps cannot fully do so yet. In fact, I`m not sure you could locate its birthplace very accurately anywhere. However, later when I visited Toledo and Córdoba in Spain I learned of the wonderful cultural mix of Muslim, Jew and Christian that had prevailed there for a time. There, Islamic scholars like Averroës who had access to Arabic versions of the classical literature of ancient Greece and Rome, lost to Europe in the Dark Ages, translated them back and gave us access to these treasures. Spain`s power later spread into and overwhelmed northern Italy for a time, probably bringing these texts along with them.

We did not for a moment think we had "done" Florence but we had already had a full day and wanted to get back to our peaceful estate and perhaps a game of tennis. On driving out of the covered car park I looked both ways and pulled into the street, suddenly noticing as I did so a young woman on a scooter whom I had come close to hitting. I don`t know yet whether she had suddenly pulled out from somewhere, whether she was in a blind spot or what, but she yelled at me and waved a fist as I turned. The incident shook me and restored the total caution and alertness of my first day in the country.

We headed back but somewhere took a wrong turning and found ourselves in a small town we had not expected to be in. We could find no signs either that told us where we were or how to get back to anywhere we recognized. I stopped the car in a quiet street and looked at the map with Malcolm to try to identify where we could have gone wrong. Malcolm noticed a woman coming along the street with her shopping and suggested we ask her. I agreed that was a good plan as long as she spoke English. Malcolm delicately asked if all my years of interest in Italian opera had taught me nothing that could be of any use. I wondered. I knew how to say "your tiny hand is frozen" and "women are fickle". Neither seemed helpful. I thought further. I could manage "when the stars were brightly shining", "on with the motley" and "no, I am not a clown." Malcolm looked unimpressed and the lady was coming closer. Suddenly I remembered "dove sono" from Mozart`s Marriage of Figaro. That means "where am I?" That was better. From Rigoletto I recalled "pari siamo" meaning "we are the same." I leaned out of the window and established she did not speak English. I said "dove siamo?" She gave us a name which we could not immediately find on the map. From somewhere else I remembered "ah, che voglio" which was something about "I want". I said "voglio Pontassieve" since we knew how to navigate from there. She smiled, nodded and then burst into floods of Italian for which my operatic knowledge was no help at all. We caught "rivoltare", "sinistra" and what sounded like "semaforo". That was accompanied by typically extravagant hand gestures. We nodded and said "grazie", each of us hoping the other had grasped a little more than we knew we had. We decided "rivoltare" did not mean she was revolted by us since she kept smiling. More like a suggestion to turn round. "Sinistra",I felt sure meant left or on the left. The word "semaforo" puzzled us. We felt it unlikely that anyone was practicing semaphore signalling in the main street of wherever we were. Malcolm wondered if it could mean some other kind of signal like a traffic light. This was such a good idea that I felt sure we had to turn round, go to the traffic lights and turn left. I turned the car and drove in the direction she had pointed. We prayed for traffic lights and, there they were. We turned left and noticed a sign ahead. We approached it and, sure enough, we were on our way to Pontassieve. "Maybe opera`s not so useless after all," Malcolm generously admitted.

We only had a week in Tuscany and we didn`t want to spend it all in the car. We had an ill-advised walk down the steep hill, past the olive groves to the little town of Pelago. I only say "ill-advised" because it was so hot, and if going down the hill was an effort we were not going to enjoy coming back up. The town is attractive with a large main square and cafés where we could shelter. However, one other trip we had decided on was Siena. Many books described it as more wonderful than Florence and its cathedral was one of the most celebrated. The walk to Pelago had quite reconciled us to the thought of 40 miles in an air-conditioned car. Our first dilemma on reaching the city was parking. The guide book had warned us that the historic centre was no place to leave a vehicle. We probably erred on the side of caution and had another walk in the sun that we might have saved ourselves. Once we reached the old part however the tall, ancient walls offered plenty of shade.

We had lunch beside the old arcade and already admired the buildings. Siena is often compared with Florence but in fact its heyday was earlier, and the main part of the old centre dates from the 14th century. Over lunch we discussed an item Malcolm had read somewhere that Italians had some of the worst table manners in Europe. We had not noticed this by that time (nor have I noticed it since). However, we did see a couple of businessmen enjoying bowls of pasta with their chins more or less on the table. Malcolm suggested this might be the source of the reputation. However, rather than bad table manners this seemed like good sense. It was difficult to move that kind of food any distance without dropping something on the very fine suits they were wearing.

The famous Piazza del Campo was only a short distance away. It is best known as the setting for the famous breakneck horse race "the Palio" which is held there twice a year. For a mere 90 seconds brightly clad riders from each of the city`s 17 traditional districts or *contrade* hurtle around the specially built tracks with most of the city in attendance. We had missed this spectacle by a few days but were not especially sorry about that since that would not be the best time to see the other features of the place. The piazza itself, often cited as the most beautiful in Italy, is laid out in nine sections of red brick with the august town hall, the Palazzo Publico, on one side. I believe its tower, the Torre del Mangia, is the second highest mediaeval tower ever built in Italy. They are constructed mostly in warm red brick and look in remarkable condition for having been built in 1342.

We headed for the Duomo, Siena's famous cathedral. I am often surprised by explorers who want to see outer space or the depths of the oceans, normally incurring considerable cost and expending a lot of effort. Unless they had a very unusual upbringing they would be likely to see more to astonish them simply by walking into a building like this. It has sculpture, paintings and a form of architecture that combines Romanesque and Gothic elements. In it are the works of Pisano, Donatello and Michelangelo. There are 56 inlaid marble scenes created over a 200 year period by some of Italy's greatest artists. But into all of this very Italian magnificence come black and white striped pillars, Bernini's golden lantern and the blue dome with stars. This brings more than a breath of the orient, perhaps the palace of a sultan. I don't suppose there is another building like it even in Italy.

One of the highlights for anyone of the cathedral is the Piccolomini library, containing the frescoes by Pinturicchio of the life of Pope Pius II. For Scots however there is a particular treat. The painter depicts an incident in his earlier life before he became Pope. As Aeneas Piccolomini he was sent by the Pope on a mission to Scotland to meet James I. Pinturicchio of course had never been to Scotland, and might have been hard pressed to find anyone who had been. This is rather obvious from his depiction of the meeting. King James and his courtiers are shown groomed like Hollywood superstars, sitting in a hall with marble pillars straight from Carrara. The countryside looks pretty much like our Tuscan hillside at Castiglionchio and you feel a quality Barolo is about to be served, perhaps with very un-Scottish grapes and even a fresh Gorgonzola. What adds to the amusement is that the former Pope, who was something of a wordsmith, left a description of Scotland which the painter either did not read or found so unattractive that he preferred to ignore it. Aeneas had described a cold country with no trees. The men spent their time digging black rock out of the ground to burn. He thought the people quite likeable but was much more aware of their use of rough animal hide than quality fabrics from Milan. He will not have seen marble pillars and the king would not have looked as if his wardrobe was from Bulgari. It is not recorded whether he was offered a bowl of porridge or a taste of the haggis.

By now we felt we had earned another ice cream. We had noticed a shop on our way to the square so we retraced our steps and found a vendor of what looked and tasted like quality ice cream. Only as we strolled back out of the historic centre towards the car did I reflect on how much I had been charged for this treat. It was a lot. I have checked my change a little more carefully in Italy ever since. This tendency is by no means universal but nor is it wholly uncommon.

We felt we had used our week well. Italy had certainly not disappointed. It was the first of now many visits I have made to it, stunned each time by the variety and beauty of the place.

Robert Noble Graham

SKIRTING THE UNDERWORLD, SAILING TO CAPRI FROM SORRENTO

I might have loved Sorrento for its name alone. As a little boy I used to listen with my spellbound mother whenever the radio played the great Italian tenor Beniamino Gigli singing "Torna a Surriento", (Come back to Sorrento). We lived in Partick, in post- war Glasgow, at the time when bombsites were a common feature. I was quite surprised when I was old enough to travel to see that most cities did not have unattached walls standing beside heaps of rubble. I had assumed it was an essential feature of modern town planning, although at the age of four my grasp of that subject was elementary at best. However, the idea of singing with such romantic vehemence "Come back to Partick" even then seemed to me improbable. This had to be some special place. There was no question that the song was further enhanced by the beautiful but totally unintelligible words:

Vir 'o mare quant'è bello,
Ispira tantu sentimento,
Comme tu a chi tiene a' mente,
Ca scetato 'o faie sunnà.
Guarda gua' chistu ciardino;
Siente, sie' sti sciure arance:

Later, when I learned the Italian language I was disappointed to realise that the song was still unintelligible. Something about the beautiful sea and somebody smelling as nice as an orange was all I could make out. The reason for that is that it`s not really in Italian but in Neapolitan dialect. I suppose that as a child in war- ration Glasgow the notion of anyone smelling like an orange would have seemed as alien as the language. In fact the idea of anyone even owning an orange would have been a novelty. I had spent most of the first two years of my life in a hospital for sick children so I expected people to smell of things like disinfectant and cough syrup.

So I learned to love the song very early and grew up with the conviction that Sorrento was a faraway place where the sun shone a lot, people smelled like oranges and disembodied men with loud voices enchanted my mother. I still love the song but am better informed about the place now that I have visited it.

I was running my own business around the time of the millenium and I had come through a difficult winter. I had been faced with a huge tax bill which my accountant had somehow failed to anticipate, followed by an expensive family difficulty, followed by the realisation that my business associate of the time had been swindling me for a year or more. I needed something to restore me.

Robert Noble Graham

Perhaps some unconscious association of my emotional state with the bombed-out Glasgow of my childhood suggested Sorrento as the place one went back to. A more immediate reason was that I was going abroad in February and there are not many parts of the European mainland where I`d have a chance of sunshine. I confronted my business associate and was taken aback when he did not deny having swindled me. He also could not quite grasp what was wrong with continuing this practice which he found so beneficial. I was at first speechless as he expressed his exasperation that I should wish to amend the situation. Could I not see how much better his life was as a result? How was he to explain to his wife that they were to live only off the proceeds of his activities and not mine? The conversation spun further into the transcendental as he pointed out that if I persisted in this course he would have no choice but to take legal action. He took my ensuing silence as needless obstinacy and left with the ultimatum that unless I very quickly became more reasonable "action" would follow. To cut a long and scarcely believable story short, others pointed out to him that his case was not very strong. I therefore quickly received a welcome payment of most of what I should have received in the previous year. Suddenly I could afford a holiday. I decided on Sorrento.

Sorrento is a small town of perhaps 17,000 inhabitants in the Bay of Naples in the Italian province of Campania.

Archaeological and historical evidence suggests that in former times it was a significant commercial centre, trading with the Balearic Islands, North Africa and the Levant. At one time the Mediterranean was a very active trading area. At various times Egypt, the Lebanon, Turkey, Venice and Greece had been prosperous and active. Nowadays all of them are pale shadows of their former greatness with the possible exception of Turkey which is beginning to prosper again. Southern Italy, now a major headache to the prosperous north of the country as well as to the eurozone, was the resort of rich Greeks in ancient days. Plato, Aeschylus and Pythagoras all lived there for a time. Archimedes whom we usually think of as Greek was born in Syracuse, Sicily, and spent all of his life there until a Roman soldier forgot the stern order to spare the great mathematician and killed him. We might therefore think of Archimedes as Italian but all this area was part of what was known as Magna Graeca or "greater Greece" so he was Greek. The Normans in the twelfth century set up a vigorous Kingdom in southern Italy which was successful enough to draw the envious attentions of the papacy, the Hohenstaufens, the Angevin dynasty and the Spanish rulers of Aragon. This powerful realm began to crumble when Sicily seceded after the damaging Sicilian Vespers riots on which Verdi based his opera. Now Sorrento survives mostly by tourism, since it is at the head of the famed Amalfi coast which draws plenty of rich visitors.

I arranged to fly to Naples and take the bus round the bay coast road to Sorrento. The road is relatively new, skirting the terrifying volcano, Vesuvius, with the deep blue Bay of Naples on the other side, about 24 miles of dramatic splendour. I felt it would be a scenic overture to my visit. I could savour the view as my memories of Gigli`s surging voice imploring his beloved`s return to Sorrento came back to me. However, that was not what happened. I arrived at Naples to discover there was no bus. Instead, a man stood in the terminal holding a board with my name and the travel company I had used. He was a man of medium height, aged perhaps 40. He had a lot of very dark hair which flooded back from his receding hairline as if he were permanently standing in a strong wind. He wore tinted spectacles and looked at the world with an air of faint contempt.

The city of Naples is associated with many things. It had the ancient sibyl of Cuma, one of the prophetesses depicted by Michelangelo in the Sistine Chapel. Lady Hamilton and Lord Nelson spent romantic evenings there. It has the largest world heritage site of any city and produced both pizza and Sophia Loren. However, I am ashamed to admit that this surprise change of plan made me more aware of its dreadful reputation for some of the most pervasive and brutal organised crime in Italy. Had my business associate meant something rather different by `taking action` than I had supposed? Who was this man? Why was he there? I confessed to being the person he was waiting for. He explained that he was Angelo Ercolano, a taxi driver. There were no buses along the coast road because of a landslide which had blocked it. This seemed plausible. How could I argue? I was not very familiar with the local geography but it seemed to me that the taxi would have a long journey to reach Sorrento other than by the coast road. He agreed that this was the case. The major problem was that the volcano, Vesuvius, stood in the way. This turned out to be a most favourable mishap.

The journey took more than an hour and a half but Angelo proved to be a very learned guide. We set off through suburbs of Naples which Angelo described to me as "a third world land in Europe". "Very dangerous suburbs," he advised. In fact, he told me, Naples altogether was one of the loveliest, most exciting cities in Europe but one of the least safe. He confirmed that its historic centre was the largest Unesco heritage site in Europe but the dangers of being mugged were quite high. I had not planned to visit it other than that I had been told by a client that its archaeological museum was an astonishing treasure house. Angelo agreed and said it was a very short trip from the railway station, so probably well worth doing.

Robert Noble Graham

Gradually we got through the suburbs of Naples and turned south. The great bulk of Mount Vesuvius was on the right. Vesuvius is often said (probably inaccurately) to be the most active volcano in the world and is certainly one of the most dangerous. It is, really, a super volcano like Yellowstone Park in the USA. The whole area around it, including the city of Naples, is the caldera of an unstable region which is expected to erupt sometime in the next 100,000 years. From the road I could see a lake between us and the mountain with rocky islands and visible steam rising. "That is the Campi Flegri," explained Angelo, "the Phlegrean fields of Greek and Roman mythology. Virgil in the Aeneid said that was the entrance to the underworld. If you walk by that lake you will burn your feet and you will smell the sulphur. Very like Hell." Angelo realised he had a receptive audience so he opened up. He explained to me that we were in the region of Campania which had been very poor for a long time. It suffered badly during the war and in a land that loved food above almost all else there was very little to eat after 1946. His parents told him they had often had to go to bed hungry. I looked at the hillsides on the left and noticed oranges and lemons hanging on the trees. They had not been properly tended in wartime so they had not been as productive as they were now. Naples had been the strongest centre in Italy of resistance against the Nazis but had paid a high price.

Angelo advised me to visit Positano which was just down the coast from Sorrento. Evidently it has two of the world`s ten most expensive hotels and Hollywood stars can regularly be seen there. Then I should continue along the famous coastline to Amalfi and Ravello. "The views from Ravello are the best on this coast," he explained "Wagner stayed there for a time and based the magical gardens of the evil sorcerer, Klingsor, on it." There seemed to be nothing about this area that Angelo did not know. By this time we could just see the rocky white shape out in the Bay that resembled the tooth of some great monster. "That is Capri," he explained. "Ulysses came past there in Homer`s Odyssey. He was lost on the way to Ithaca and he should not have come this far. It may be the winds blew him as far as Gibraltar and he was finding his way back, looking for shelter round this coast. That is how he met the temptress, Circe, who turned his men into pigs. Circe was a siren. That is how Sorrento got its name. It is the place of the siren that almost destroyed Ulysses. "I asked him if I should be careful of the women in Sorrento then. " You should always be careful of women," he advised with barely a smile. "But especially careful here. Just north of here is Mount Circeo from which Circe would have spotted Ulysses` boat. Once the men came ashore she turned them into beasts ". I began to worry. "Ulysses resisted her because the god Hermes gave him the herb *moly* which was probably a form of garlic and that protected him." I have noticed myself how effective garlic can be at keeping women away. Angelo moved on and told me that many famous people had lived on Capri, one of the first being the Emperor Tiberius. I doubted that Tiberius could really be living on Capri while administering Rome. How would he communicate without telephone, fax or email? "Carrier pigeon," explained my encyclopaedic guide. "A pigeon can get to Rome in an hour without crashing like computers do." I asked if it was true that Tiberius had isolated himself to indulge in strange sexual practices as Robert Graves had claimed in his novel I, *Claudius.* Angelo shook his head. "I don`t think so. Tiberius was sick of Rome. He was lovesick. He had married Vipsania Aggripina as a young man. He was forced by his stepfather, Augustus, to divorce her and marry Julia the Elder. He loved Vipsania and missed her terribly. He came to hate the debauchery of Rome. He left most of the day to day administration to Sejanus who was a brute. He went to live in Rhodes soon after marrying Julia to escape Rome but returned as emperor. He moved to Capri as he became aware that his mind was going." I asked him why so many Roman emperors went mad. Tiberius was the great uncle of Nero and great, great uncle of the totally deranged Caligula. Was it simply a genetic flaw? "No, it was lead," he replied without hesitation. "They drank from pottery goblets and they always wanted new ones. The potters then used lead to make the slip they finished the pots with. If you kept using the same goblet you might survive it but if you insisted on new ones all the time you simply poisoned yourself, madness being one symptom." I thought of the condition of "potter`s grot" that had been known down the ages to describe the condition suffered by those making dishes and goblets. The potter would lose control of his limbs and eventually his mind. It was only when they discovered the dangers of lead that that stopped. This should not be confused with "potter`s rot" which resulted from prolonged exposure to the silica in clay.

We now entered the famous coast road and came into Sorrento from the south. The white cliff face of Capri looked enormous out in the blue water. "So, does the story of Scylla and Charybdis come from this channel between Capri and the mainland?" I asked, thinking again of Ulysses. Angelo shook his head. "No, that was the strait of Messina between Calabria and Sicily", he replied. "Circe also describes to Ulysses that he will pass the place of wandering rocks with tempestuous and destroying flames where the birds cannot fly in safety. That is Stromboli, the volcano that never stops erupting. You would pass it just before the strait of Messina."

We stopped in front of a large building by the sea. One of its walls was simply a continuation of the cliff face. This was the Hotel Ambasciatori where I had booked. I thanked Angelo for a remarkably interesting and entertaining journey. I was uncertain of what the payment arrangement was for this trip but Angelo assured me that had been taken care of. I gave him a tip for which he thanked me and he gave me his card. He told me he could give me a reasonable rate for a trip down the coast to Positano, Amalfi and Ravello. I told him that sounded worth doing. Later I reflected on the precarious financial position from which I had recently emerged and that my position was still hardly secure and decided not to call him. I have always, irrationally, felt a little guilty about that.

The hotel was something of a palace. I was a little surprised when the smiling receptionist confirmed that I was actually booked in there. She asked me how I`d arrived when the road was blocked. I told her I`d had the most wonderful taxi ride. She nodded in recognition.

"You are lucky. People pay a lot for Angelo`s tours. He`s very knowledgeable."

"He told me that all the women in this town are sirens. Is that true?"

She laughed.

"We do our best."

An eager young porter showed me to my room and looked at the tip I gave him as if he had never seen money before. He closed the door and I stood, a little awestruck, in my room. The door, the table and the chair were of heavy dark wood that looked freshly painted and of high quality. The floor was marble and ahead of me Venetian windows opened onto a balcony. I was fortunate to have a room with a sea view. I walked out to the sunshine and saw the deep blue water of the Bay of Naples below me. When I looked up I could see the entire panorama of the Bay. To the north at the far side was Vesuvius, now only half the mountain that erupted in 79 A.D., destroying the towns of Herculaneum and Pompeii. It is perhaps a curious fact that one of my earliest memories, along with Gigli singing, was of a photograph in a children`s encyclopaedia of Vesuvius and the article mentioning the destruction it caused. I had no idea at that time that there was any connection at all between the singing and the dreaded volcano.

The scene over the bay from a balcony such as the one I had must be one of the world`s great views. Even if you knew nothing at all about the history the sweep of land round the inlet with the volcano at its head would be arresting. Then you look out to the immense stretch of blue sea with the islands of Ischia and Procida to the north and Capri to the south on my left. Ischia is the largest of them. The English composer, Sir William Walton, moved there at the age of 54 and lived there for the last thirty years of his life with his young but highly intelligent Argentinian wife who created a famous garden at their house in La Mortella. Towards the end of his life he regretted having moved there. He complained that he had assumed the Italians to be very musical but had decided they were simply noisy, although they did have beautiful voices. Some have felt that had more to do with the increasing grumpiness that often accompanies old age than with any fault of the Italians. Probably wherever he lived he would have found the world noisier.

I was a little stunned that the fairly modest amount I had paid had secured me such a spectacular room. I was reluctant to leave it but it was early evening and I wanted to look at the town and assess how foreign it was. I also wanted to find one of the seven restaurants that had been recommended to me by an ex neighbour who was a travel manager and apparently familiar with every trattoria and pizzeria south of the Alps. I went out into a warm evening. The blue sea of the bay was on my right as I began the short walk to the town centre. It is not Rome or Florence so there are no great monuments to see. There was still some daylight which there would not have been in my Scottish home town. The major difference however was that shops, restaurants and cafés were open and most of the town`s population seemed to be outside. I was immediately struck by the fact that the majority of the people I was seeing were not only dark haired and dark-eyed, which I had expected, but were clad in expensive looking black leather. Italian style is famous and I have no doubt these people had paid a lot for their jackets, coats and boots but the effect was of an eccentric school uniform.

I continued along the pedestrian walkway until I found the Sorrento restaurant which had been recommended to me. It was empty of guests. A small, dark-haired man stood surveying carefully set tables with subdued lighting under scenes of the Amalfi coast, like a great banquet set out for guests whose invitations had never arrived. He showed no impatience, like these soldiers you read about in ancient epics who continued to guard their post long after the town had been sacked, the king deposed and the wine cellars drained. The stalwart guard would man his post all the more nobly for the extreme futility of it. I realised I was allotting a poetic grandeur to the waiter that was not really deserved. It was simply early in the evening and I had no doubt he would soon be busy enough.

I greeted him in Italian, keen to get as much practice as I could in a language I wanted to speak better. He acknowledged my greeting in Italian and then invited me in English to take a seat. His English was correct enough but he spoke with a heavy accent that was not Italian.

"Vous êtes français?" I asked. "Canadien," he replied. We both smiled, I took a seat and we continued our conversation in a mixture of French and English. I asked him how come he was living in Sorrento. The unsurprising answer was that he had met a woman here while on holiday. I thought of Angelo`s warning about the sirens but thought it better not to raise the subject. I asked how he liked living in this very different environment. He said he liked it but had never entirely adapted. He told me he missed seasons. Whilst visitors were enchanted to see lemons on the trees and blue sky he felt he would appreciate it more if there had been a couple of months of ice and snow. I understood, but since I had just come from the chill of a Scottish winter along with an icy phase in my personal life I could only rejoice at the early spring.

There was music playing as I perused the menu. I looked at the waiter.

"What is that piece of music?" I asked. "I`ve heard it several times lately but I don`t know what it is."

"That`s Caruso," he replied.

"I know Caruso. That`s not him."

He laughed.

"It`s the name of the song, not the singer, although it is about the singer."

"It`s a beautiful song. There can`t be many songs about a singer."

I knew that Enrico Caruso was something of a local hero, although long dead. My mother loved the singing of Gigli but some of her brothers maintained he could not compare with Caruso. Caruso had been born in Naples in 1873. He had gone on to become the most famous singer in the world and the first major star of the gramophone age. He was particularly well received in New York but toured widely including places like Mexico City, Uruguay and Argentina. He would never consent to perform in his native city however after having been treated cruelly by an audience in his early years. He said he would only ever come back to Naples "for pasta". He was an affable, good-natured man who was well-liked by fellow performers. There is a story that he ran into the great Irish tenor John MacCormack one morning in New York and asked heartily "So, how is the world`s greatest tenor this morning?" to which the Irishman replied:"And since when did you become a baritone?" In fact, Caruso, rather like Placido Domingo, was a tenor who could sing baritone. Once, during a performance of "La Bohème" at the Metropolitan in New York his good friend, the baritone Antonio Scotti lost his voice when coming up for the famous "overcoat" aria. Caruso whispered to him to mime. The audience heard a fine baritone performance of the aria, most not aware that Caruso, out of clear view of most of them, was performing the piece. He made an enormous amount of money before his very untimely death at the age of only 48. Who can say if he was greater than Gigli or more recent tenors like Domingo or Pavarotti? There are plenty of his recordings still available and he was clearly a very fine singer, but the quality is not good enough to make fair comparisons.

"Well, it is a love song," explained the waiter." It is supposed to be the words of Caruso to a woman he loved. He sings them, knowing he was dying. It`s a bit controversial. They`re very passionate words. You`d assume it was a woman he was having an affair with but in fact they were probably addressed to his daughter. It`s very popular here. There`s a museum to him at the Caruso restaurant in the town."

I have subsequently heard the song several times performed by Pavarotti, Josef Calleja and Kathryn Jenkins. Only recently I heard it sung by the composer, Lucio Dalla. I was surprised. He was clearly not a conventionally trained singer like the others but in fact it`s perhaps the most moving performance of them all.

I soon decided that Sorrento was a pleasant and picturesque base but not worth a lot of my time. The day after my arrival I walked down to the jetty to take the hydrofoil to Capri. It was a sunny day. The sky and sea were blue and the high walls of the island looked very near. I was not alone as I waited. There were clearly a few tourists like myself including an unhappy looking American couple. They were both quite short and round. The man wore a brilliantly red denim shirt which he appeared to have bought when he weighed three stones less. On his worried looking head he wore a grey baseball cap and his trousers were a pale mauve colour. It was difficult to believe his outfit had not been carefully chosen to defy and offend all notions of sartorial elegance. By contrast, a short man of around the same age, perhaps fifty, wore a matching suit and trilby of charcoal grey with fine threads of blue and gold delicately traced through. His shirt was indigo and appeared to be made of silk as was his golden tie with navy stripes. He had a bushy, carefully groomed moustache and his black shoes shone. Every finger of each hand, apart from the thumb, had a ring that looked like gold. He smoked a thick cigar as he paced regally up and down, chattering away delightedly. He was accompanied by two taller, thick-set young men who looked as if no joke had ever penetrated to the depths of their sombre souls. The man chatted to them, smiling at his own conversation which he clearly found scintillating. No doubt he was the local plumber, but it was difficult not to have thoughts of godfathers and men with impressive powers of persuasion. I decided that I was unlikely to seek out the company of either the American or the stylish Italian. I did however have the sobering thought that the American struck me as possibly a factory worker or shopkeeper who had worked hard and blamelessly all his life and was now having the European holiday he and his wife had dreamt of. I felt the Italian`s earnings were possibly of a more questionable if more substantial nature. In a just world the American would have been the happier man, but that did not appear to be the case. I hoped my analysis was wrong and that each had the satisfaction their deeds had earned, but I thought it unlikely. I did toy with the intriguing question whether the main object of each man when he had chosen his attire that morning was to be noticed. If so, both, in their wildly different ways, had succeeded admirably. I then wondered whether having been noticed had enhanced their lives in any important way.

Eventually the hydrofoil arrived. It was larger than I had expected and accommodated us all quite easily. I had not particularly wanted the company either of the Americans or the stylish Italian and I was able to take a window seat on my own. I sat and watched the blue water of the bay with an innocent and peaceful- looking Vesuvius in the distance. As I sat in thought a waiter came around offering coffee. Since I had no idea when my next shot of caffeine would be I accepted. It was hot, strong and very good. The Italians just have some very high standards for some things. The hydrofoil, like the boats, comes in at the very busy port of Marina Grande. The great pale rock towers upwards over the small harbour teeming with visitors. As we waited at the head of the stairway to disembark I saw the godfather still chattering delightedly as the Americans, rather like the Italian's two companions, regarded the island with stony expressions as if queuing for prison.

The sun was now high in the sky and pleasantly warm. I found the milling crowds stimulating rather than oppressive and I always find the Italian language delightful. I once read that the poet T.S. Eliot, even when he knew no Italian, realised that Dante Alighieri was a great poet with the first incomprehensible line of his work he read. I've often wondered if, when he knew the language better, he would have given the same accolade to the entire population. I have heard plumbers clearing drains uttering musical language in Italian streets. Dante was a very great poet, but I feel he had a head start over the bards of more pedestrian tongues.

Guidebooks advise that a funicular will take you from Marina Grande up to Capri, the larger of the two small towns on the island. I used to believe that this was the funicular made famous in the song *Funiculi,Funicula* but in fact that celebrated the opening in 1880 of the one going up Mount Vesuvius. Unfortunately it was destroyed by the eruption of 1944. The song became immensely famous and was recorded by artistes as different as

Luciano Pavarotti and Alvin and the Chipmunks. It also led to the great German composer, Richard Strauss, being sued. Strauss had believed it was a traditional Neapolitan song created by someone long dead and forgotten so he used the theme in his tone poem, *Aus Italien.* In fact the song had been specifically written for the opening in 1880 with words by the journalist Peppino Turcino and music by Luigi Denza. Denza took Strauss to court and was granted a share of royalties. Later on both Rimsky Korsakov and Arnold Schoenberg used the melody with no litigious consequences.

Unfortunately the funicular was out of service on the day we arrived. The American couple looked, if anything, even more dejected than before. I didn`t see the godfather but I imagined he had more stylish and personal transport available. There was a line of taxis by the funicular entrance and I saw the Americans go off to interrogate one. I decided to provide myself with some fruit and perhaps a Panini and walk up to Villa Jovis, the best known of the many villas Tiberius had built on Capri. It sits on the top of the 334 metre high rock tower that dominates the north east of the island. That is not actually the highest point. Monte Solaro in Anacapri to the west is higher. Apparently the dramatic cable car to that was working but I had made my decision. The climb to Capri was quite steep but there was a good road. I stopped in the stylish, affluent little town for a last shot of caffeine before going further and then set off.

I had first heard of Capri as a child. At that time one of the most famous UK entertainers was a singer from Rochdale named Gracie Fields. She was a very fine singer but also had a very engaging personality. She lived much of her later life on the island, initially prompted by the fact that her second husband, an Italian, would have been interned if they had attempted to live in Britain during the Second World War. She grew to love her island home which she referred to as "Rochdale by the Sea." She later lived there with her third husband, a Bulgarian radio repair man. Her magnificent house was visited by many stars such as Noel Coward, Richard Burton and Elizabeth Taylor. The great Russian ballet dancer Rudolf Nureyev had also owned a house on the island but rarely occupied it.

The walk was immensely rewarding. The sea views on either side were magnificent and I did not tire of the sight of lemon and orange groves on the hillsides with fruit heavy on them. This was likely to take up most of my day and I soon realised how foolish I had been to imagine I`d also have time to take the bus to Anacapri, the island`s second town in the western, quieter part of the island. I should like to have seen some of the churches, especially San Michele which has a spectacular majolica floor depicting The Earthly Paradise".

Robert Noble Graham

The walk up to Villa Jovis became very steep towards the end and the villa is in a poor state. However, the views all around were spellbinding. We were surrounded by deep blue sea under the cloudless sky. Vesuvius sat in innocent tranquillity across the bay and I could see over the main body of the island sufficiently to catch part of the Amalfi coast. I could not fault Tiberius`s taste from the point of view of scenery. I did wonder how he passed the time in such a remote spot. Even assuming Suetonius and Graves were correct about his erotic exploits there must have been hours that were difficult to fill. He was emperor of course so there would have been affairs of state, but unless the air was permanently thick with carrier pigeons there can`t have been that much to do. If he enjoyed vigorous walks there would have been no shortage of them but that might have become more difficult as he aged and wrecked his system with aphrodisiacs and lead-contaminated wine. There are always voices warning us of the corrupting influence of technological advances but I can only conclude people with this view are very poorly informed about how corrupt the world was and still often is in the absence of such distractions. You don`t have to know very much history about anywhere to realise that violence and degradation were commonplace in most societies who did not have enough to entertain them.

I walked around and shortly was joined by the American couple who arrived by taxi. Lunch had not made them any more sociable and they still avoided eye contact with me. I had seen all I wanted to by this time anyway. I decided to set off downhill and, if possible, find a good spot with a view to have something to eat. The taxi driver gave me an expectant look as if hoping for a fare back down to the town, but I signalled to him that I was walking and he shot off in what seemed like an irritable manner, but perhaps he always drove like that. I soon found a good spot since the descent was much quicker than going up. There was a viewpoint almost directly below Villa Jovis from which I could see one side of it if I looked up. There was a convenient block of stone that served as armchair and table and I had my humble repast, finishing with a ripe banana. When lunch was finished I went over to the two iron bars of the fence which prevented people from hurtling down the cliff face and dropped the banana skin down into the sea. As I did so, I heard a yell from above me. It was the doleful American, evidently outraged at my act. I smiled and shouted "It`s a banana skin." I had assumed this would set his mind at rest but I was wrong. "A banana skin, so!" he replied as if expecting to see hordes of poisoned marine creatures immediately washed up on the shore. He could hardly have been more outraged if he had caught me dumping nuclear waste. I wondered if American bananas were toxic. "So it`s bio-degradable," I added helpfully. "Bio-degradable!" he sneered, like James Bond saving the planet from Smersh (banana flavour). I was just wondering how much elementary biology I could condense into one sentence to ease his mind when his wife said something to him. It might not have been "you thick bozo, that`s how the planet survives," but it was clearly something equally stunning. He glared at her like a man whose world has just ended and then turned away.

I made my way down and returned to Sorrento. That evening I went out to one of the restaurants my neighbour had recommended to me. It had the striking name of `O Parruchiano`. It`s one of the largest restaurants I`ve ever been in and since it was off-season it felt like dining alone in Wembley Stadium. I had a very tasty casserole which was, I gathered, traditional in Campania. It was cooked very slowly, using some of the cheapest cuts of beef along with chopped pork sausage. I might not have ordered it if I had known more about it, but in fact it was delicious. I also ordered one of the local reds that had been recommended to me and drank all of it, thus ensuring a headache before breakfast. The day had been a great success and I ended it by planning some more trips from Sorrento.

For much of the year you could simply enjoy the sunshine, food and wine by the Bay of Naples, but it is a centre for a number of more or less mandatory journeys. I decided that even with the small amount of time remaining to me

I was going to have at least an initial look. First of all, the Amalfi Coast summoned. I could have hired a car or, if my finances had been less rocky, I could have telephoned the omniscient Angelo. Even the briefest look dissuaded me from driving on that cliff-edge road so I decided to trust the bus. This was a good decision for a number of reasons. A passenger can, of course, see much more than a driver,

and being a little higher up could only be a benefit. Part of the beauty of the coast is its restless twisting and turning with different panoramas of the sea opening as you travel. I was sitting close to the front of the bus and at first was a little alarmed on seeing cars hurtling towards us on a road which, particularly in the tunnels, was barely more than single track. However, my esteem for the bus driver, and even for the average Italian motorist, rose as I saw the patience and judgement with which they manoeuvred, reversing when necessary.

Of course, one of the great sights on this trip is the view of the little town of Positano which perches on the edge of the rock, looking as if perpetually tumbling into the sea. The main street through it was certainly not designed for buses or motorised transport in general, but, remarkably, it now tolerates a lot of it. On we went to the coast`s largest town, Amalfi. Amalfi is very beautiful, sitting at the foot of a high ravine. Nowadays it is a minor town, well known for tourism, some of the best lemons anywhere and a liqueur made from these lemons. Its cathedral is majestic with the celebrated *Chiostro del Paradiso*, a magnificent cloister showing the influence of Islamic architecture. The cathedral is dedicated to Saint Andrew, coincidentally both the patron saint of Amalfi and of Scotland. The saint`s connection with Amalfi arose from the fact that Amalfian mariners, during the times of the town`s power, brought what they claimed to be the saint`s bones from the Middle East. In former times Amalfi`s importance was far greater. Between the 7th and 11th centuries it was a major maritime power, rivalling the influence of Genoa. It was using coins for trade at a time when others were still bartering. Its maritime tables were used far and wide by mariners and it is thought to have used the first mariner`s compass in Europe. Its arsenal constructed some of the most powerful ships of the Mediterranean and its wealth was enviable. However, the harbour was badly damaged by a tsunami in 1343 but by that time its power had been greatly reduced by the Norman kingdom of King Roger of Naples, assisted by the Pisans who were jealous of Amalfi`s success. It has never regained any of that influence.

I rhapsodised about the view from my hotel room on arrival. Of course a major feature of that view was the sight of Vesuvius across the bay, and still one of the most

Coffee, Chianti and Caravaggio

striking images of my visit was the smoke and steam arising from the area around the volcano`s foot at the Campi Flegri. I had first read about its destructive power in an encyclopaedia when I was a child. Now I had the opportunity to visit the scenes of Herculaneum and Pompeii, the two major towns destroyed by the eruption of 79 A.D.

I decided on Pompeii first of all. A regular train left from Sorrento on the *linea circumvesiana* and I took it after breakfast. The train was quite full and I sat opposite a man and a woman. He was perhaps 50 with close – cropped hair and thick-rimmed spectacles. She was around the same age with sand-coloured hair tied severely back. Both looked thoughtful, even worried. I was aware of them looking at me as I sat down. I momentarily wondered if the seat was taken but I saw no reserved notice or evidence of occupancy. The man continued to watch me with a face that wandered between expressionless and questioning. The woman gazed out of the window as if my sitting opposite them was a problem beyond her powers of comprehension. Eventually the man leaned forward and I realised he was about to speak to me. What would he say? Would he tell me that for some reason I had no right to be on this train? Would he tell me that for some reason my presence was upsetting to him and his wife. I looked at him, puzzled, expectant. With some difficulty he finally said the word :

"Pompeii?"

I wondered if this was the password for some secret society devoted to occupying seats on trains. I felt that unlikely.

"That's where I'm going," I advised, hoping this reply would get us somewhere.

He nodded as if I had introduced a novel idea. He looked at his wife who continued to gaze fixedly out of the window.

"Dreadful. Quite dreadful," he muttered. I nodded, hoping I was agreeing to something for which my agreement was welcome. He settled back, evidently feeling we had explored the subject in full. The train trundled on up the coast, heading for the famous volcano. After a silence of ten minutes or more he leaned forward again. I hoped he would seem a little less conspiratorial.

"We find it very moving. We come here frequently. We never get used to it. Dreadful, just dreadful. "

"It's my first visit."

He turned to his wife:

"His first visit," he repeated. At first she showed no reaction and then in a quiet voice she said:

"Dreadful, just dreadful."

I began to wonder if this visit was wise. Would I be haunted by its images night and day for the rest of my life? Would I too feel compelled to return as they seemed to do to be tormented once more by the scene? Was I volunteering for an existence haunted by ancient volcanic outpourings?

As we reached the station I found myself leaving the train with an anxiety I had not felt on setting out. I decided to avoid the doleful couple if possible and make up my own mind about Pompeii. In fact the scene struck me as far from dreadful. I entered *Porta Marina* after a short walk from the station. This is the usual entrance and was so-called because it faced the sea which, before 79 A.D. was only 80 metres away. The site is much larger than I had expected with the sea on one side and Vesuvius in the distance. The sun was shining out of a blue sky and my first thought was what a splendid place Pompeii must have been before the eruption of 79 A.D. Enough of it remains to give the impression of a prosperous city by the sea with wide streets and squares, impressive villas and the remains of shops and offices. The western area particularly has been uncovered in reasonable condition. Unlike Herculaneum which I would see later Pompeii was destroyed by hot ash and pumice-stone. The inhabitants were mostly killed by the fast-moving pyroclastic cloud which would have brought debris with it. In Herculaneum mud slides were the killer, one reason the town is better preserved. What we see of these towns now is the result of a long period of careful excavation which began in 1748. The process has not finished, particularly in Herculaneum.

As a settlement Pompeii is ancient. The first recorded population is of Oscans in the 5th century B.C although it seems likely that Etruscans and Greeks also had a presence there. It is not very clear who the Oscans were but linguistic evidence suggests they may have come from Umbria further north. They seem to have warred unsuccessfully with local Samnites who became the dominant local force. Squabbles with local tribes continued with periodic appeals by one or the other for Rome to intervene. The Romans seem to have done so a little half-heartedly, partly because they found the place unhealthy. Malaria was common then. It killed four popes and Saint Augustine along with many others. It was a more effective deterrent than wild tribesmen. One attraction to the mighty rulers apparently was the lascivious lifestyle of the Oscans. Roman generals often enjoyed a lively orgy, especially far from spying eyes in Rome. However, it was not until 80 B.C. that the great Imperial Power totally absorbed Pompeii. Even when they did they appeared to take great care to preserve the distinguished houses, theatres, law courts and basilica, a surprising amount of which buildings remain more or less recognisable.

I strolled around the remains of Pompeii, struck by very human details such as the block between *Quadrivio di Olcona* and *Via Meridionale*. Here you find the *Fullonica* or laundry beside *The House of Verecundus*, a clothes factory and *The House of the Lararium* with a counter which had large holes in it. These were to enable the merchant to place sizeable vases or urns of delicacies to be sold to customers. When excavated, some coins were found on the counter, placed by someone anticipating a mouthwatering snack, entirely unaware of the disaster about to engulf him. The long *Via dell`Abbondanza* was lined with inns for the population and visitors. The *Macellum* is still recognisable as a wide market-place where many transactions must have taken place before business colleagues retired to one of the hostelries. There was of course a theatre, baths and a brothel retaining detailed murals of some of the services on offer. I happened upon *The Antiquarium*, a visitor centre where a glass cabinet displayed some of the human figures unearthed. These are in fact casts made from the space in the ash and lava where a body would have been. I was a little taken aback to see a number of Japanese visitors photographing them avidly. My first reaction was that this was ghoulish. However, when I considered later that Japan has around 10% of the world`s active volcanoes and that many of them are near population centres I decided their interest in the phenomenon was likely to be more urgent than mine.

The experience of Herculaneum is quite different. The site is not as immediately impressive as Pompeii since it is effectively a suburb of Naples rather than an open area by the sea. Much has still to be excavated, but most of that lies under housing currently in use. No doubt the Neapolitan authorities have some plan for re-housing and further excavation but it looks problematic. Since Herculaneum did not suffer the same pyroclastic bombardment as Pompeii most of the buildings are intact. On arriving I saw nowhere to buy a booklet such as had helped me to understand Pompeii, but I noticed a group just a little ahead of me who clearly had a very entertaining guide, judging by the laughter. I approached and gathered that the tour was being conducted in French. It was a rather eccentric form of the language however which was explained when I understood that the man was from Naples so, although his French was fluent, he was not a native speaker. I joined him just as he was explaining to his group his view of how wasteful modern society was. "You piss and you flush it all away because you are embarrassed by it. We can only do that because of the saintly Englishman, Thomas Crapper, who invented the siphon toilet disposal (*actually this is not true. The flushing toilet was invented by John Harrington in 1596 but Thomas Crapper was a plumber who, in 1868, started his own company which marketed and publicised the invention far and wide)*. I do not blame the great Thomas Crapper. I have two shrines to him in my own house because I too am a modern man. In Herculaneum and Pompeii however the piss was collected and treated with proper importance. Why did they do that? Were they just vulgar Italians like my neighbours in Naples who piss against the walls? No. They were modern-minded, environmentally friendly Italians we should be proud of. They saved the piss to cure animal hides to make the excellent leather the elegant ladies and gentlemen would wear. It was a most valuable commodity. "

The guide seemed lively and no one objected to my sudden appearance in the group. We were then led to one of the cobbled streets where our attention was drawn to runnels on each side.

"So why do we have these grooves in the streets of Herculaneum? Note that approaching the road intersections   they go gently uphill to disappear at the junction. Why was that? Did the workmen just get tired? Ladies and gentlemen, this is where ancient Herculaneum was centuries ahead of modern Naples. The wealthy people and the trades people travelled in carriages or carts with big wheels. The distance between the wheels across the cart was exactly the distance between these grooves. So the cart would run smoothly along the street but, approaching the intersection, the horse would slow down because he was going uphill and would come to a halt at the junction where the grooves ran out. They didn`t have traffic lights in those days so this was their solution to ensure they didn`t have collisions at every junction. In modern Naples we have traffic lights. But Naples is the most democratic city in the world so the driver who arrives at a red traffic light believes he has the same right to go forward as the one who comes up to a green traffic light. If he happens to be behind a misguided tourist who has stopped at the red traffic light he will get out and wave his fist at him until he moves. For that reason we have lots of collisions at junctions in Naples, but they are very advanced, democratic collisions. We should be proud of them too. Italians have a lot to be proud of."

I followed the group to the end. I had missed some of the earlier descriptions but I had seen and heard enough to recognise that, like Pompeii, Herculaneum had been a civilised, well functioning city brought to a sudden, disastrous end. I thought once more of the extent to which yesterday`s unthinkable catastrophes become a source of interest and tourist revenue for succeeding generations.

My time in the Campania sunshine was running out. I had another excellent meal with a bottle of local wine beside the bay. As I ate and drank and enjoyed the scene I felt satisfaction that I now had ample reason to come back to Sorrento as the great Gigli had urged, although his plea was no doubt directed at someone more beguiling than myself. I knew there was a great deal more to this area than I had explored. I knew for instance that the hills behind the town were criss-crossed with an intricate network of pathways used in former times before motorised transport was possible. They lead to an ancient, self-contained world less dramatic than volcanic eruptions or the journeys of Odysseus, but fascinating in their own way. I thought I heard recently that the well known broadcaster and former politician, David Mellor, always holidays in Sorrento. Whilst I doubt if I would ever want to confine myself to one area of the world Sorrento would not be at all a bad choice if I had to.

Robert Noble Graham

THE OVERWHELMING CITY -ROME

On my second trip to Rome I was accompanied by my daughter, Abi, on her 19th birthday. We had made a memorable visit to Paris when she was 17 so Rome seemed a reasonable choice for this one. My first encounter with the Eternal City had been in January a couple of years before and I had been dazzled by it. I wondered how I would react this time and how my daughter would. I was a little cautious since I had had personal experience of Stendhal`s syndrome. The famous French novelist (real name Henri Marie Bayle) was a great lover of Italy, but even he reported in the early 19th century that any traveller who tried to see more than a little of Rome at any one time would experience headaches and dizziness and feel decidedly unwell.

I had booked us rooms at the Art Deco hotel in Via Palestro. It is well situated, just ten minutes walk from the main railway station which you come into from the airport. I was also intrigued by the name. Amid the treasures amassed under both temporal and papal power in the city of emperors and popes the idea of Art Deco was so democratic and functional that I was intrigued. I thought of the Chrysler Building in New York and the Champs-Elysées theatre in Paris. The spirit of Le Corbusier and his followers seemed very out of keeping with the world of Michelangelo, Raphael and Leonardo.

It was late afternoon when we checked in. The hotel had been well named. We saw bright colours along with geometric designs. There were bold scenes on the walls more evocative of young, energetic America than of the ancient European seat of imperial power. The ambience was friendly and welcoming. The rooms were quite small but perfectly good for our needs

It was early September so the city was still bright and warm, but cooler than the burning months of high summer and less overrun with visitors. We were eager to explore. I suggested we walk down Via Cavour for a first sight of ancient Rome, the Forum and the Colosseum. Almost immediately you are surrounded by grandeur. Even the doors of private apartment blocks are made of richly varnished oak and are big enough for a chariot to get through. In a sense, choosing Via Cavour was an irony after my thoughts of Rome as the great imperial city. Camillo Benso, count of Cavour, was the first Prime Minister of the united Italy. It arose in 1861 after centuries when the country had been a collection of city states. These, at various times, had come under the power of Austria, Spain, France or even in ancient times, Greece. Cavour, as he is generally known, was a liberal Piedmontese politician who died at the early age of only

51, a few months after the declaration of the country's unity. He was clearly a very remarkable man who, incredibly, was placed in a military academy when only ten years old. He survived being punished with a bread and water diet for reading "the wrong sort of books". These appear not to have been early versions of Playboy or even Batman, but rather weighty volumes by British philosophers such as Jeremy Bentham and John Stuart Mill. This gave him a high opinion of British political thinking which, sadly, did not survive a visit to England where he found its reality more depressing. The English have their belief that in its time of direst need King Arthur will once more move among them. I have often wondered what good a mediaeval knight clanking through the corridors of Westminster could do, however charismatic, especially since his brand of English would not get him an A level. He did have this excellent party trick of drawing big swords from stones and then hurling them into lakes for a magic hand to grasp. Not entirely clear what impact that would have on unemployment or inflation. On the whole I felt the talents of Cavour were more obviously helpful to a modern state, especially the one he was so instrumental in founding. I sense that recent Italian politicians have not been his equal. Incredibly and sadly, Rome, the great imperial city, was still not part of that united country during his lifetime. It continued for a time to be under the rule of France, only liberated in 1870, 9 years after the death of Cavour.

Abi and I stopped at a bar in Piazza d`Esquilino, near the great basilica, Santa Maria Maggiore, the only place in the world, I believe, where mass has been celebrated daily since the 5th century. Its site, allegedly, was chosen by Pope Liberius on 5th August AD 352 when the Virgin Mary appeared to him and suggested he build a cathedral on the area where the snow would fall on the following day, a most unusual occurrence in a Roman summer. I have never seen a snowfall in Rome, but I assume it is quite unlike what we have in Scotland where the same instruction would lead to a church which would dwarf the Vatican and quite a large part of Italy along with it. At this stage I didn`t go into rhapsodies with Abi about this wonderful building. I did, however, point out that a few yards from its august entrance was the best ice cream shop I have ever found.

Abi had by then decided on her career path as a physicist. She had little of the dewy-eyed romanticism of her father who finds poetry in ancient languages and glamour in largely dysfunctional old cities. From an early age she had shown a remarkable understanding of engines and gadgets. Whenever, in her early years, we were puzzled how to operate a new food processor or egg- whisk we would simply hand it to Abi in her pram and her tiny fingers would fit it all together. Whilst eager to see the wonders of Rome she was also interested in establishing a programme of research, preferably one in which we could find common ground. This turned out not to be difficult since we had both been much exercised by the question of whether pizzas made in a wood-fired oven were inherently better than those fired in less traditional facilities. We decided there could hardly be a better laboratory for this research than Rome itself.

My general experience of catering in Rome is of friendly, jovial waiters, but occasionally I`ve been in ones which had a faint air of menace. The one we had stopped at was one of these. It had very small windows, and the clientele were mostly either solitary males or small groups who spoke in hushed voices. A small, balding, thick-set waiter patrolled watchfully as if weapons might appear. I concluded that it was simply an old-fashioned hostelry that served the working men of the city, and had no particular interest in attracting tourists or stylish professionals. I decided this was more likely than my sinister imaginings.

We headed down Via Cavour which leads to the Via dei Fori Imperiali. There the ruins of the Roman forums are spread out spaciously. The church of Santa Maria in Aracoeli and the Capitoline museums stood on the hill to our right, just beyond Trajan`s column. To our left was the

Arch of Constantine and the damaged mass of the Colosseum. It was one of these Roman scenes that pay homage to ancient Greece. The Romans displaced Greece as a military power and evidently did not rate them highly in that regard. However, their reverence for Hellenic architecture and creative imagination was unbounded. Anyone familiar with the buildings of Periclean Athens like the Parthenon or the huge temples of the former Greek colony of Sicily can recognise the mark they made on Italy`s capital.

Near the bottom of Via Cavour we had noted a restaurant with the sign "forno di legno" (wood-burning oven). This was our chance to begin our research project. First of all we strolled by the forums on the far side where the road skirts the Circo Massimo by the Aventine Hill. The Circo Massimo was an arena once capable of seating 30,000 people. They would mostly gather to watch chariot racing. Its last recorded use was under Totila the Ostrogoth in 549 AD when the glory of Rome had passed. Totila is generally regarded as one of the Germanic rabble that destroyed the seat of Empire but in fact he was better than that. Not only a very skilled military leader and successor to the mighty Theodoric the Great, his principles suggested he might have got on very well with Camillo Benso, Count of Cavour. He believed in liberating slaves and distributing land to peasants. I don`t know where these notions came from since he would not have had the benefit of reading Jeremy Bentham and John Stuart Mill. What is true is that such consideration for followers was not unusual amongst ancient Germanic tribes as anyone who has read the Nibelungenlied will confirm. My early schooling had taught me that civilisation had succumbed to undisciplined hordes when Rome fell. I came to believe this was perhaps not accurate. It would, after all, not be difficult to improve on a society whose Saturday afternoon entertainment was watching Christians publicly devoured by lions.

A slim, smiling young waiter welcomed us to the restaurant. It gave the illusion of being a small, intimate establishment by having several rooms, each of which had only a few tables. However, we realised later that there were several of these rooms and the total complement could be quite large. We ordered our pizzas and waited with an anticipation that was as academic as it was gastronomic. We would satisfy the higher intellectual hunger along with the mere appetite. I had chosen a seafood topping and Abi had gone for one of the assortments that had pieces of mortadella, pepper and artichoke. We decided on a glass of house red which we felt was a necessary element of the atmosphere. Eventually they arrived and we watched like starved refugees as the sizeable offerings were placed before us. Immediately we saw the thin pastry, blackened in places as is to be expected from the genuine wood-fired oven. Abi took her first bite and looked at me.

"Daddy, this is the real deal. I suspect the debate is settled. "

"Thin evidence so far", I suggested.

"Thin pastry. Just the way it should be. "

I finished cutting my pizza and had my first mouthful. I could only agree. It was excellent. The topping also had that full, fresh-herb flavour of quality cuisine. We felt we would have to think of a different project for the week.

The following day we decided on a major assault on Imperial Rome. We headed from our hotel in Via Palestro down the Via XX September, down the Quirinale hill. We turned off at Via Barberini to the Fontana dei Tritone, better known to the world as The Trevi Fountain. This, too, stirred memories of my young years. In 1954 the American film "Three Coins in the Fountain" appeared, one of many Hollywood creations that depict Europe as glamorous, crumbling and populated entirely by gigolos. The theme song from it, sung by Frank Sinatra, is a very fine song and was the first introduction for many people to the valuable information that throwing coins in Roman fountains was a reliable way of finding enduring love. A few years later a film named "La Dolce Vita" appeared, directed by Federico Fellini. It made a star of a Swedish blonde named Anita Ekberg. The film was a sensation, partly because Ekberg, while wearing a kitten on her head, wandered fully clothed into the fountain at midnight to the surprise of her companion, Marcello Mastroiani. At her request he waded in too in his Italian suit. This was so different from the behaviour of John Wayne and Humphrey Bogart in American films that everything Italian was then seen as the way to go.

The Trevi Fountain is magnificent, allegedly named after Trivia, the young lady who first drew the attention of thirsty Roman soldiers to the cool stream. Rather more plausibly, it drew its name from its site at the meeting of three roads (*tre vie*).   I have been to it several times, and if the legend about it is true then enduring love would appear to be more common than I thought since it is always mobbed. We then headed for the Spanish steps, so called because they lead down to the Piazza di Spagne where the Spanish Ambassador to the Vatican lived. The steps are broad and stately, often decked out with huge bunches of flowers. The large square at the top of them is usually occupied by artists of varying quality. We were taken by the work of one who had done a tiny water colour of the Caffé de la Pace, the oldest in Rome. We bought it and made a note to visit the café later. It sits as a secret for the few in a secluded alley behind the Piazza Navona.

When you come down the steps into the Piazza di Spagne there are two places of interest for an English visitor (we were not and are not English but of such wide, all-embracing culture that we were intrigued). One is the museum devoted to Shelley and Keats. In fact it also contains material about Wordsworth, the Brownings, Oscar Wilde and the ubiquitous Byron. Keats died of tuberculosis in the house at the age of 25. He had been extremely ill before leaving England and the aim of the trip had been to expose him to the warmer Italian climate. Delays meant they didn`t reach the city until late November by which time it was not warm at all. His weakened condition was probably not helped by his doctor`s insistence that he eat no more each day than a piece of bread with one anchovy. I feel unwell thinking about it. The use of the house as a museum to the English bards was largely owing to the efforts in 1903 of the American poet Robert Underwood Johnson.

On the other side of the steps is the more cheering Babington Tea House. This was opened in 1893 by two English ladies, Isobel Cargill and Anne Marie Babington, to serve the large English population of the city. Nowadays its clientele is by no means confined to the English. It is a very elegant establishment, serving a large variety of high quality teas with food of various types. They will, for example, do a full English breakfast of eggs and sausages or for American tastes they will do pancakes with maple syrup. It is not however an obvious stop for the budget traveller. The prices are quite high.

On this visit Abi and I didn`t linger at either of these sites. Threatening clouds were gathering and we wanted to cross the Tiber to reach the Vatican. We headed along the straight road that begins as Via Condotti, past the expensive Bulgari and Armani shops. As it changed to Via Font Borghese heavy drops began to fall. We broke into a run and we were not alone in rushing across the river at the Ponte Umberto as lightning flashes worthy of the great city tore the sky apart. We were all headed for the stout fortress Castel Sant`Angelo, round, ageless and sturdy, on the far bank. As we hurried in torrents of rain water were flooding out. We galloped up the stairs to the uppermost gallery which went round the building. There we stood in a small river, but at least it was heading down the stairs and slopes to the street outside. We could hardly see Rome for the curtain of rain that was falling. Jupiter sent some mighty lightning bolts as well, making the point that he may have been replaced as a god in the Roman mind by cappuccino and Versace but he could still put on a show.

We decided with clouds still lingering it was not a day to stand in the long queue for the Vatican museums. We left the Castel Sant`Angelo with steam rising from the streets and were vastly outnumbered by nuns and priests as we headed for Saint Peter`s. The Via della Conciliazione which leads up to the immense edifice is broad and welcoming. The crowds in Piazza San Pietro were smaller than usual, perhaps because of the recent downpour, and we made our way under the eyes of the statues of saints on top of the huge porticos to the basilica. According to tradition St.Peter was crucified in the Circus of Nero in AD 64. In AD 324 Constantine ordered the building of a basilica over the tomb. It was then rebuilt in the 15th century but then various architects laboured through the 16th and 17th century to construct the current immense edifice, inaugurated in 1626. At that time the then pope, Urban VIII, commissioned Bernini to design the Baroque canopy over the tomb. This is known as the baldacchino , and its pillars twist ornately upward below the overarching dome of Michelangelo. This was my second visit to St.Peter`s but Abi`s first. I felt no more able than I had on my first sight of it to know what to think of its vast, opulent magnificence. Again, as before, what really touched and moved me was the Pietá of Michelangelo showing Mary holding the broken body of her son. She looks delicate, tragic, vulnerable, symbol of all of humanity down the ages, helpless before the awfulness of mindless destruction. I have no doubt that St. Peter`s alone could induce a severe attack of Stendhal`s syndrome if not taken in measured doses over a long time.

We left and went into the first reasonable- looking trattoria for a late lunch. Our waiter welcomed us with the delight of a man who had waited years for just this moment. He was a medium sized fellow with receding dark hair. He wore large spectacles behind which his eyes bounced with surprising merriment. I had by now taken some Italian lessons and seized opportunities to practise it. I was helped in this aim by this jovial waiter who finished every sentence for me as soon as I had managed the first few words. This did make him feel I was saying things I had never intended to say, but whatever he was inventing seemed to make our welcome visit an increasing joy and delight for him. We ordered lasagne. This was Abi`s first experience of the fact that pasta dishes in Italy often come with a lot of pasta and very little filling. This contrasts with my local café in Dunfermline which does the dish with prime beef mince encased in thin strips of pasta, a very fine treat. Our Roman lasagne did however come with a large helping of very fresh basil which you would be much less likely to get in the UK.

We spent that afternoon strolling down the west bank of the Tiber. The river itself is not particularly impressive, but it is lined by so many marvellous buildings that there is plenty to admire. We detoured to look at Rome`s largest landscaped park, the 1.8 square kilometres of the Doria Pamphilia gardens. These date from 1630 when a man with the unlikely name of Pamphili Pamphilia acquired land in the area. He quickly extended it by buying neighbouring vineyards. The property became known as the *Bel respiro* or "beautiful breath" since it was on relatively high ground and free from the "bad air" or *malaria* which, as we know, brought deadly disease. The grounds were made considerably more grand when Giambattista Pamphili became Pope, adopting the inappropriate name of Innocent X, possibly exhibiting a taste for pontifical irony. He is the subject of a famous portrait by Velazquez in which the great Spanish portraitist depicted a man whom you might well have employed to prosecute bitter legal disputes for you but probably not as a spiritual adviser. He neither looked like nor behaved like a man who trusted God to achieve very much. The Pamphili line died out in 1760. The then Pope Clement XIII allocated the lands to Prince Andrea IV Doria on rather tenuous marital grounds. Clement was not entirely misnamed, being of an affable disposition, always anxious to please. His major flaw was rampant nepotism in which he was not alone in Vatican history (or indeed the history of power anywhere else). The park is now owned by the City of Rome.

We did not spend very long in this estate before realising it was a recipe for Stendhal syndrome with blisters. Whatever muscle or nerve cluster is responsible for the feeling of awe soon felt overworked as we eyed the palaces, statues and bridges produced for the wealthy family over several centuries. Our tour was brief, noting that Rome was great for palaces but poor for good quality grass, as we strolled across bare patches in the lawns. We were kept alert by armies of intense joggers who showed even less interest in magnificent edifices than we were doing. They pounded along with eyes downcast, proving that mankind will provide itself with pain and suffering if there are no Neros or Caligulas around to do it for them.

The day was wearing on and we now made for Trastevere, one of the oldest parts of the city whose inhabitants, it is said, consider themselves to be the only true Romans. This is probably not accurate, since it was colonised by Etruscans from the 8th century BC, and was only conquered much later by Rome and brought under its rule in the reign of Augustus.   In the main I think of it as a fine antidote to the relentless life-enhancing experiences of the Eternal City. Trastevere is more restful with its many excellent restaurants and its little cobbled alleys. However, being Roman, it does have some magnificent sights as we discovered on reaching Piazza Santa Maria in Trastevere just when daylight was fading. The square was lit by the glow from the 12th century mosaics, now floodlit, on Rome`s oldest church, probably dating from the 3d century AD when Roman Emperors were still pagan. That sentence should be read with some scepticism since I think there is very little evidence that Roman emperors ever found any more spiritual illumination in Christianity than in the worship of their household gods. Their faith was in anything that could go some way to ensuring their survival and that of their various, sometimes rather basic, pleasures. It seems likely that Constantine's conversion was largely a political manoeuvre. A religion that encouraged people to be humble and obedient and not be very troublesome was much more attractive than others that encouraged world conquest. The Germanic notions of fearless warfare leading to heaven as Valhalla where there was more endless warfare must have been quite alarming.

We admired Santa Maria in Trastevere in the evening glow. The sight was lovely. After that we were ready to turn our minds to the serious project of our week. We now had to find a restaurant offering pizzas made in any kind of oven that was not wood-burning. This proved to be very easy to do. Just a hundred metres or so away in Via San Francisco da Ripa we found a large traditional trattoria whose range of pizzas was bewildering. Although we felt the question was decided in favour of wood-fired ovens it was important, for intellectual honesty, to sample the alternative. This seemed just the place to do it. The quiet, dignified waiter, who looked as if he hadn't slept for days, soberly took our order and we waited. He brought us each a glass of house wine and we discussed the day's events as we waited. The restaurant was quite busy but it had a pleasant atmosphere of Italians eating out. No doubt there were also tourists but they merged easily with the natives.

Our pizzas looked magnificent as they arrived. The tension was palpable as each of us thoughtfully cut our first segment. Together we tasted it. We looked at each other. Perhaps the matter was not settled at all. We would never have mistaken this for a pizza from a wood-fired oven, but it was delicious. In its own way it was just as memorable.

We took a different route the following day. First of all, we took Via Cavour again but this time stopped at the extraordinary basilica, Santa Maria Maggiore. It is properly termed a basilica, in fact a major basilica, since it is one of the four buildings which have this designation by papal decree. The others are St.Peter`s, St. John Lateran and St. Paul outside the walls. At one time the four together with St. Lawrence outside the walls represented the five patriarchates. Santa Maria Maggiore represented the patriarchate of Antioch. The basilica dates from the fifth century and was built under Pope Sixtus III. It is the largest of Rome`s so-called Marian churches, those dedicated to the Virgin. This approach to Christianity was particularly strong after the Council of Ephesus in 431. There are those who would argue that the emphasis on Mary was to encourage the conversion of Middle Eastern peoples who had worshipped a female deity such as Astarte, otherwise known as Isis. This is reminiscent of

George Bernard Shaw`s view that "the conversion of a pagan to Christianity was the conversion of Christianity to paganism." Other views were that Mary was seen as a particularly suitable deity for carrying the imperial memories of pre-Christian Rome along with those of the adopted religion. I cannot myself understand this argument but no doubt a few years of intensive theological training would make all clear to me. I find it curious that a female deity was so widely worshipped in the Middle East in ancient times. Was it some kind of manic reaction to this that gave us the rampantly patriarchal religions that came out of it subsequently?

What is totally clear to me is the immense effect of Santa Maria Maggiore. I would not say that that effect is especially spiritual, unworldly or Christian. You could equally say that it is a wonderful example of how material things and worldly aims can be fashioned by human genius to produce great beauty and magnificence. From the fifth century there are 36 mosaics which depict the lives of Abraham, Isaac, Jacob and Moses. These are framed by 40 columns from the same period. There are further mosaics in the loggia and on the triumphal arch and more in the 13th century apse. The ceiling is coffered and gilded with what is said to be the first gold brought from the New World by Columbus. Older than any of this and of great meaning to the church is the icon of Mary which is in the Borghese chapel of the basilica. The building is huge, and as you go through its many treasures and down the steps to its origins it appears to be a church that unites pre and post Christian, east and west and includes influences from ancient Greece, the Middle East and Africa. To someone of no religious affiliation it still gives an enormous sense of the vision and creativity of mankind during times when military destruction and disease were prevalent. You don`t need to have any particular dogma to be impressed by the basilica as a triumph of the creative spirit over destruction and of perpetual renewal in a dangerous world. The sheer beauty of much of the interior is absorbing and uplifting to anyone with eyes to see.

To regain our sense of perspective after one of the undisputed wonders of civilisation we had an ice cream. Not perhaps a wonder, but certainly one of the best of its kind either of us had ever tasted. I wanted to visit the Terme di Caracalla. These are the most magnificent of the baths created in Rome. They were begun in AD 206 by Septimius Severus and completed 11 years later by his son, Caracalla. In fact his name was not Caracalla at all but Marcus Aurelius Septimius Severus. Apparently the nickname came from a cloak he had been given after a Gaulish expedition. Caracalla was an extremely unpleasant man who happily authorised murders including that of his brother, Geta. I find it hard to believe he would have been happy with a nickname like that. I`d be surprised if a tyrant like Hitler or Saddam would have enjoyed a nickname like Anorack or Duffel-coat. The Terme when new could, apparently accommodate 1600 people and probably served more as an informal meeting area than necessarily for personal hygiene.

I wanted to see the baths as a result of the first "Three Tenors "concert of Carreras, Domingo and Pavarotti. It had been broadcast from the Caracalla baths in 1990. The mighty trio were all football lovers who were in Rome for the World Cup. Carreras suggested the concert and it was speedily organised. For that occasion the baths were beautifully lit, and on a summer night in Rome with a large audience it seemed such an impressive setting. We took a complicated route but a scenic and historic one, down Via Cavour, along beside the forums, past the Colosseum and down past the Circo Massimo. The baths are now a major tourist destination. They are partially ruined, but much of the edifice remains intact. It was odd to see it in reality. Not only had it been skilfully lit when the concert was broadcast but the magnificent music and singing had given it an aura of romance and passion. The ruin we saw had certain grandeur, but deprived of the colour and music it was a more forbidding presence where the dark spirit of Caracalla appeared to brood more sullenly.

We now walked back towards the Tiber and reached the attractive little mediaeval church of Santa Maria in Cosmedin, another of the `Marian` churches, furthering the cult of the Virgin. Attractive as it is, it is better known for the Bocca della Veritá outside it. In English this would be called "the mouth of truth". It is a large, circular image of a face, probably that of a pagan god like Oceanus. It`s often thought to be the God of the Tiber. It is a large image with the diameter of a grown man. The mouth of the face is open. This enabled it to be used in the middle ages as a test of lying. If you put your hand into the mouth and told a lie your hand would be bitten off. Conveniently, no one was ever asked to explain the actual mechanics of this process. Obviously whatever did the biting would have to be quite vicious and partial to human flesh. However, it would have to be sufficiently intelligent to be able to discriminate between truth and lies. Given that it was so intelligent how could it abide such an uninteresting way of passing the time? I`m not aware that anyone has tried to explain such matters.

As our final day approached Rome still had abundant treasures we had not discovered. We could have visited the Palazzo Borghese with its marvellous Bernini and Canova sculptures, or Santa Maria del Popolo with magnificent Caravaggio paintings of St. Paul and St. Peter. We could have sought out one of the city`s finest wine shops and savoured Italian vintages for hours. What we did resulted not only in appreciating some of the great cultural treasures but provided an unforgettable culinary experience as well.

We headed first of all for Piazza Navona. This magnificent baroque square is as authentic a heart as the city can claim. Around Bernini`s wonderful fountains are cafés and trattorias where Romans and visitors, businessmen and academics interact. The layout of it is basically the stadium built in the first century A.D. by Domitian. Its name supposedly comes from the story that Saint Agnes in AD 304 was stripped naked there and martyred for refusing to marry a pagan. Borromini`s statue Sant`Agnese in Agona commemorates this and the current name is thought to be a corruption of Piazza d`Agona. It is also important for being the starting point for the rebirth of the city. Rome was in spectacular decline at the end of the fourteenth century when the Papacy moved to Avignon in The Great Schism. This lasted from 1378 to 1417. Even today much of the wealth and importance of the city comes from the Papacy and its loss was nearly fatal to it. Its return and regrowth resulted from a succession of Popes who would not have been out of place in any organised crime syndicate. Martin V, a Roman and a member of the powerful Colonna family, in 1417 initiated the return. He was a formidable administrator and a sufficiently fearsome man that the lawlessness into which the city was sinking was checked and reversed. He expelled the market from Piazza Navona and began the construction of the great palaces and churches which now surround it. He was followed by Eugenius IV who found Rome so frightening that he lived in Florence whilst his brutal bishop, Vitelleschi, destroyed, slaughtered, hanged or decapitated any obstacle, animate or otherwise, that threatened the renaissance of the city. He met his end by poisoning, probably administered indirectly by Eugenius. Sixtus IV, after whom the Sistine Chapel is named, took office in 1471 and instituted widespread reconstruction, at times pillaging ancient Rome, the forum and the Colosseum to do so. He had been born in poverty but had no intention of returning to it. He would have taken a dim view of the teachings of St. Francis of Assisi who embraced poverty as a blessing. He too practised nepotism more than any normal religious observance and showered gold on his nephew who was to become Julius II, the one for whom Michelangelo created the great tomb in San Pietro in Vincoli on the Esquiline Hill. Julius, even while Pope, loved nothing better than a good war. His spirits rose when he had the chance to jump on a horse and ride off for an invigorating day of bloodletting and butchery. It is difficult not to be repelled by such figures but without them we could probably not have the eternal city we now enjoy.

After looking round the square we visited the Caffé de la Pace, Rome`s oldest. It sits in a small open space in a narrow street just behind Piazza Navona. It was a warm morning and there were tables placed invitingly outside. Sitting in the sunshine in Rome with coffee and excellent company is a pleasure difficult to match. With a high wall on one side and a tall church tower behind there was a sense of quiet seclusion that contrasted well with the crowds in Piazza Navona. I asked for filter coffee but the dark-haired young lady explained patiently to me that they only did coffee. Before learning something of Italian attitudes I might have found that answer confusing. She was gently telling me that true Italians do not simply consider mutations such as filter coffee, Americano, latte or whatever to be inferior products. They simply do not regard them as coffee at all. We decided to have coffee and she nodded in acknowledgement that this was a wise choice. I have noticed that this attitude has softened a little in recent years, no doubt under the pressure of tourism. After all, if foreigners wish to delude themselves that they are having coffee with these peculiar beverages why should their money not be accepted. The true Italian can continue to enjoy coffee.

Next we headed through the Piazza di Sant` Eustacchio to a building that had survived intact all of the fluctuations in Rome`s fortunes. We were moving into the financial district and the political one where the Stock Exchange is situated and the ephemera of daily life are carried out. Beside it all however is the Pantheon. Even in Rome this is a uniquely impressive building. What stands there now is mainly the construction under Hadrian in 126 A.D. but that replaced one built under Marcus Agrippa in 30 BC, probably to much the same design. The principal reason for the Pantheon's impressiveness is that it is topped by what, even 2000 years after its construction, is the largest unreinforced concrete dome in the world. It has a central opening to the sky known as the *oculus*. The height to the oculus and the diameter of the interior circle are the same at 43.3 metres. The weight of this dome is, apparently, 4,353 metric tons.I assume the similarity of the numbers in the height and the metric weight are a coincidence but it is a striking one. The ceiling is coffered. The building greatly influenced Brunelleschi when he designed the dome for St. Peter's and the building has been described as architecturally the most influential ever constructed.

The Pantheon has had several uses since its construction, mainly as a Christian church. The great Raphael and the composer Albinoni are buried there. The name is Greek for "all the gods" so perhaps in conception it was the most tolerant and all-embracing of the world's religious buildings. Whether because of the great uncluttered space inside it, the geometrical harmony or the imposing figures in the niches around the wall the Pantheon does have a great sense of majesty. There is probably no other building like it.

It was now time for lunch. We were hungry and went into the first eating place we could find. We could not have been more fortunate. In the next street was the restaurant *Armando al Pantheone*. When we went in we were quietly welcomed by a man who could quite credibly have wandered out of one of the seminaries. He was not especially tall, but very lean. His large dark eyes gazed with saintly resignation out of his lantern-jawed face beneath a large but neat mop of black hair. His waistcoat in gold criss-crossed with black lines would have been uncomfortably tight on any normally slim frame but on his it was slack. I wondered if close proximity with sumptuous Roman food was a penance of an especially refined nature after weeks of bread and water. He held his pale bony fingers in an attitude of earnest supplication as we asked if we might have lunch. He bowed his head almost imperceptibly and with a slow, elegant sweep of one of the delicate hands he indicated a table for two in polished wood. The restaurant was quiet. The room we had entered was like an ante-room for a wider one further back. On the other side of it were a couple of businessmen in stylish Italian suits, both in their fifties or older. They were well through a bottle of white wine with very little food in evidence. There was a small piece of cheese on a plate but nothing more.

We considered the antipastis. I chose whitebait and Abi, somewhat to my surprise, chose the marinaded vegetables. Our gaunt waiter glided off, hardly seeming to make contact with the marble floor. Then he returned, took a plate from one of the wooden cupboards and opened another by lifting a trap door over a kind of sink which held the marinade. He used a draining spoon with slow, graceful flourishes as if saying a benediction. He closed the door, stood for what seemed like a prayerful moment and placed the dish before Abi. She waited with admirable restraint until my whitebait arrived. We began. Almost immediately Abi put her fork down and looked up at me. What was wrong? I looked at her.

"Daddy, you have to taste this." I did. It was perhaps the most delicious thing I have ever eaten. The vegetables were unremarkable. There was onion, pepper, courgette, spring onions, cauliflower and broccoli. Something in the marinade was quite wonderful. We should have asked what was in it. Would they have told us? I don`t know. Since that time I have tried every recipe I can find. Without exception they have been good, but none has really approached that exquisite taste. Did our ethereal waiter impart celestial goodness to the mixture or is there some other ingredient I have not guessed at? Will I ever know? The rest of the meal was splendid but I honestly cannot remember what we had. However good, it was overshadowed by that wonderful first course.

It was fitting that our last day should have such a moment. We strolled off after lunch in warm sunshine. We went to the Vatican museums and got in after no more than 15 minutes. Normally it takes far longer. The Vatican museums take you along one vast corridor after another, all hung with priceless tapestries and hosting display cabinets with every kind of treasure. Our dreamy, satisfied, after-lunch mood was not really equal to the occasion. Only when we stood before Raphael's great canvas "The School of Athens" did we briefly come back to life. The figures of Plato and Aristotle are majestic and there is such a sense of dynamism as they stroll out to the assorted thinkers and artists around them that it took even our sleepy attention. After the abundant and unbelievable store of worldly treasures we had passed it was odd that the strongest sense of unworldly and spiritual attainment came from a painting of a pagan scene.

I don't think we succumbed to Stendhal's syndrome, but we were aware that we were leaving Rome with most of it still unseen. I think it is one of the world's great inexhaustible cities like London and Paris so there are always plenty of reasons to return and I'm sure I shall.

Robert Noble Graham

THE LAND OF PRINCES AND SECRET WINES -LIGURIA

I suppose I had known the placename, "Liguria" for most of my life, but until my decision to visit it I could have done no better than venture that it was somewhere in Italy. Frankly, I would not have been surprised to learn that it was really a stylish area of Croatia or even Bosnia Herzegovina.

This confusion was dispelled when I had an opportunity to join a holiday group going to "Liguria – The Italian Riviera". On further reading I discovered that the name referred to the north-western coastal strip of Italy, running from Ventimiglia on the French-Italian border to the port of Lerici south of Genoa. The term `Riviera`, to someone of my generation, conjured up various images, mostly from the 50s. An aged Winston Churchill, mercifully too early for invasive journalism, would travel there, probably already ailing from dementia. The condition was no doubt aggravated by unending amounts of cherry brandy. Brigitte Bardot distracted the traumatised French from the humiliations of occupation to remind us that her country had contributions to a peacetime world that hungered to be reminded of pleasure. In previous generations it had been the playground of princes, a term that suggests a more dashing, inspiring lifestyle than seems likely when you have seen the dull-eyed, overweight aristocrats in question. In Ian Fleming's first Bond novel, *Casino Royale*, the casino is located in the fictional town of Royale –les-Eaux, somewhere on the French Riviera. The 2006 film with Daniel Craig transplanted the action very effectively to Montenegro. It was also the setting for F. Scott Fitzgerald's novel *Tender is the Night*, based largely on his disastrous, alcoholic marriage to Zelda Sayre.

All of these associations were, of course, with the French Riviera which I had thought the only one. It seemed a little mischievous of the Italians to suggest they had one as well. By my age you realise that being wrong is an integral and inalienable part of being alive. I sometimes think, paraphrasing what John Maynard Keynes said of economists, that the world divides into those who are wrong and those who realise they are wrong. Most of the world's troubles come from people who never doubt they are right.

In fact the term "Riviera" properly belongs to all of that coastal strip that runs from South East France to the southern part of the Gulf of Genoa. What characterises and unites it is probably the best climate in Europe. It is never too hot in summer nor too cold in winter and that has been its main attraction. That feature was largely discovered and publicised by an 18th century Scottish doctor named Tobias Smollett. He recommended it to his patients for relief of most of their ailments. Anyone who thinks that name sounds familiar for some reason has probably encountered Dr. Smollett as the inventive author of the rollicking novels *The Adventures of Roderick Random*, *The Adventures of Peregrine Pickle* and his best work *The Expedition of Humphrey Clinker*. His books still sell today, although not in the numbers of James Bond. Smollett was one of these amazing people who would hardly be possible today. He studied medicine but then, without bothering to take a degree, he practised surgery for the navy. I was unable to establish whether anyone ever survived his attentions in an age before antibiotics, anaesthesia and counselling. He was well versed in Greek and mathematics and after travelling to France and Spain he felt himself competent to translate from both languages. Whist living in London he associated with great figures of his age such as Dr. Johnson and Oliver Goldsmith. He was a generous host who offered guests `beer, pudding and potatoes, port punch and Calvert`s entire butt-beer`. He was also the editor of several political journals and general editor of an immense *Universal History* in 54 volumes and later undertook to write an eight volume book entitled *The State of All Nations*. He was just undertaking a 36 volume translation of all the works of Voltaire when he died of tubercolosis at the age of 50 in Liguria.

Coffee, Chianti and Caravaggio

Our group flew to Genoa and were taken by bus to San Lorenzo al Mare. The hotel was modern and magnificently sited on the beach of the Cote d`Azur, Costa Azzurra when you are on the Italian side. It means of course, The Blue Coast, and from our hotel it was not difficult to see why as we gazed out of our windows at the Mediterranean. There didn`t appear to be much more to San Lorenzo al Mar until a few of us strolled along an unpromising road by the sea. We went past clusters of moored yachts such as I had seen in so many South European seafronts. It was not easy to work out how those moored close to the land could possibly get past the 40 rows of similarly immovable yachts to reach the sea. I suppose if you are trying to impress people with the casually dropped mention of your boat you`re not obliged to confirm that you could not conceivably sail it anywhere. I`ve never belonged to a yacht club but I`ve been told that in many rugby clubs only a minority have ever played the game. The attraction of membership is to drink with other men who live either in dreams or memories of sporting glory or who simply like avoiding their wives. I was once told that most of Bermuda was administered from their yacht club. Perhaps owning a yacht is simply the entrance fee to a mysterious inner circle of fat old men who drink gin.

We shortly arrived at a little bridge over a small stream. A stout plank of wood could have done the job for anyone beyond the age of 80 unable to step over a little water.

However, this was Italy. Some local architect with dreams of Brunelleschi had designed a masterpiece of variegated stone with white coping. It was a little bridge with fantasies of being one of the wonders of the Renaissance. We continued into the town. A humble main street was enhanced by ochre, white and blue buildings. Housewives who clearly frequented Bulgari were doing their shopping. Sun-tanned, slim men whose clothes looked new enough still to have the label on, chatted in the street, occasionally smoothing pencil-thin moustaches. Their intense, urgent discussions probably involved no more than an altered bus timetable.

Oddly, our first excursion took us out of Italy to Monaco. I had previously visited the principality and had marvelled at how the Grimaldi family had manipulated the surrounding tyrants of France, Genoa, Sardinia and Arragon to secure that priceless couple of square kilometres which, with a population of 37,000 or so is the most densely populated country in the world. The name Monaco allegedly comes from the Greek *monoikos*, meaning `one house`. It is said that the demi-god Hercules took a fancy to the place and built a house there. Since even ancient heroes did not enjoy living next to an Arnold Schwarzenegger look-alike who spent his afternoons slaying many-headed monsters, being attacked by Stymphalian birds or having the cattle of Geryon stampeding through the crocusses no one was inclined to move into the neighbourhood. Coincidentally, when Francesco Grimaldi, known as Il Malizia (the evil one) seized the fortress on the rock to wrest power from the Republic of Genoa he did so dressed as a monk. The Italian for monk is `monaco`.

For some reason we were provided with another guide on this trip in addition to our normal one, Marella. This lady, Betty, from some English provincial town, was thought appropriate to accompany us to what had once been a scene of bitterness, intrigue, struggles and naked power. I think we soon realised why. Let me say that many women who have perhaps put on a few pounds over the years can nonetheless be very attractive. This was not the case with Betty. Equally, spectacles have adorned some great beauties down the years but Betty appeared to use hers like a secret weapon with which she drilled malign gazes into her charges —us. As she got on board and cast her first accusing looks over us I wondered if Il Malizia had had some little `malizias`, one of whom may have run off to Scunthorpe and bred. Had she somehow put the `grim` into Grimaldi? Had Hercules escaped the many-headed Hydra only to be confronted by Betty? I suppressed these unworthy thoughts as we travelled towards the French border with beautiful coastal scenery around us. Betty took the microphone and gave us some interesting background. All seemed well until we approached Roquebrunne, the high hill above Cape Martin. From it the view down to Monaco below is magnificent. No tourist would want to miss the chance to photograph it. As the bus climbed to the highest point of the road Betty addressed us in the sombre tone generals must have used at the Normandy landings. She was willing, she allowed, to have the driver stop the bus but only on condition that no one, absolutely no one, should venture to cross the road. It was, she maintained, a deadly highway with cars hurtling as if from nowhere to mow down unsuspecting tourists. I don`t think I was the only one of the group to cast an eye over the surrounding landscape for bleached skeletons dangling from the trees. Nor was I the only one who had not noticed Maseratis or Lamborghinis hurtling to fatal encounters, but my senses were perhaps blunted by a drop in caffeine levels. The bus stopped and out we piled. We looked down to the high apartment blocks of the Principality gleaming white in the morning sun. Behind them the Mediterranean stretched in endless serene blue. Yachts large and small nudged each other down in the harbour with open-air cafés lining the sea. There was a moment`s silence for this tiny shrine to celebrity and extreme wealth. Then, after a collective gasp an even greater, hushed, expectant, terrified silence followed. Helen, one of our group, had daintily skipped across the entirely deserted road and was now standing at the far edge taking priceless photographs. Betty`s spectacles of implacable hostility were turned mercilessly toward her. Confrontation was unavoidable. I who, as a child, felt anxious when the Flowerpot men raised their voices, preferred not to witness the scene. There was a definite atmosphere as everyone boarded the bus once more. We descended the long hill into Monaco and were then shepherded in frosty fashion by Betty who had, I gathered, been informed that we were adults who could do interesting things like joined-up writing and look both ways when crossing roads.

I opted out of the trip to the castle since I had seen it before. I was more interested in visiting the Cousteau Oceanographic Museum. This was founded in 1910 by Prince Albert I but its director from 1957 to 1988 was the celebrated French oceanographer, Jacques-Yves Cousteau. The building itself stands majestically on the top of a cliff by the sea. Cousteau had been a major presence on UK TV when I was young. With his specially equipped research boat, Calypso, and his loyal, multi-talented crew he filmed the birth rites of billions of squid, most of which were instantly devoured by predators, followed sharks and sperm whales, filmed the mysterious sea turtles and travelled across oceans and even on Lake Titicaca in Peru. He had served in the French navy during the war and had been involved in a number of successful actions, especially against the Italians in the Mediterranean. He also was one of the pioneers of undersea equipment such as the aqualung. The founder of the museum, Prince Albert I, was quite an effective undersea explorer himself and part of the museum is devoted to his discoveries and achievements. One of its most striking exhibits is an enormous giant squid. Whether it is a brilliant model or a stuffed version of the real thing I`m not sure, but it inspires awe, both for its own enormous dimensions and also for those of the whales inside whose gut they have sometimes been found.

Monaco itself I find surprisingly uninteresting. The view from the top of the museum is impressive, although the customary harbour full of boats is given additional oddity by the extravagant hugeness of some of the craft. Wonderful I suppose, but frankly I was more impressed by the squid.

I went to the restaurant at the top of the museum for lunch and was pleasantly surprised to find other members of our group. The menu was good and I had my second ever taste of John Dory. I had always thought that a peculiar name for a fish and had assumed that some famous Cornish fisherman with that name had been the first to land one. In fact it is simply an anglicisation of the French *jaune dorée*, `golden yellow`. At least this is my favourite of the several fanciful origins I have come across. I had previously tasted it in Paris served with a cumin sauce which I found quite unpleasant. The one I had in Monaco was, first of all, much fleshier than the anorexic version I had eaten in Paris and was served with a coriander, garlic and lemon sauce that went very well indeed with it.

Next we went into France to a village called Èze. Èze is often cited as one of the most beautiful villages in France. It is certainly very pretty in itself and has magnificent views. We had been taken there specifically to visit the Fragonard perfumery, an offshoot of the main one in Grasse. We had a tour of the building. Perfumes as such are not made there. What it produces are the essences that are blended for such commercial products as *J`adore*, *Caresse* or *Belle de Nuit*. We were treated to little presentations of the art of the perfumier and informed about the wide range of essences, spices and herbs used to get the different effects. Since the time of day was less crucial for this than for a wine-tasting I was easier prey and ended up buying what I had not intended to buy. However, it served me well since I had been troubled for some time about a present for my daughter-in-law to be and this solved the problem.

We stopped again in Monaco on the way back with the suggestion that we might like to walk in the gardens, explore the casino or simply enjoy a coffee. On my previous visit I had made my first entrance to a gambling den, albeit the most prestigious one in the universe.

Apparently the rules that govern casinos the world over are devised and monitored in Monte Carlo. I had been surprised on that first visit by the extreme courtesy with which I and my companion, Audrey, had been received although we were only snooping. It soon struck me that the courtesy was good business. They didn`t know who we were. We hadn`t been dressed or groomed by anyone more exclusive than Marks and Spencer but I gather the super-rich often are not. I was also a little surprised and disappointed not to see super-heroes in tuxedos at the blackjack or bored French demi-mondaines with pearls and decolletée spinning the roulette wheel. The only punters we saw were exasperated grannies in cardigans getting rough with the fruit machines.

On this visit I discovered there was now a minimum charge for entry so that even snoopers were profitable. I suggested to my companions that the money would be better spent at the café across the square if we chose a good spot for observation. Some agreed with me. Some ventured in nonetheless. Even as we sat down a spectacle was beginning. Elegant, very young ladies displayed long shapely legs beside Alfa Romeo cars as photographers snapped them eagerly. Our table had a little frisson at one point as a red Ferrari pulled into the square in front of the casino. It was driven by a dark-haired man in a cap and shades that almost obliterated his face. The collar of his expensive leather coat was turned up to hide his neck, chin and mouth. There is a sports quiz on UK TV in which one of the challenges for the contestants is to identify a famous sports personality by an earlobe along with perhaps an elbow or kneecap. I always found it baffling, but my son was good at it. We attempted a similar challenge with this driver who had left us little more than a nose. We looked at each other. There were some suggestions it was a minor French screen idol who had once appeared with Emanuelle Beart. Clearly he needed a lot of disguise to evade detection.

A uniformed steward leapt forward to open the car door. The driver jumped out, showing himself to be no more than 5 feet 2 in height at most. He took off the cap, the shades, the scarf and the coat and stood for a moment, evidently anticipating gasps of recognition. No one gasped. None of the photographers showed any interest in snapping him. We looked at each other to ask "who the hell is that?" He snorted briefly as his pudgy little face took on a huffy look and then strode off with his tall, bored-looking girlfriend.

The following day the bus took us down the coast again, first of all to Santa Margherita Ligure from where we would take a boat to Portofino. I had never heard of Santa Margherita Ligure but it is a pleasant small town with a very scenic palmtree-lined harbour . In the centre there is a wide square with a mosaic terrace in front of the basilica of Santa Margherita Antiochia, which, I assume suggests it had links with the patriarchate of Antioch like Santa Maria Maggiore in Rome. I don't know much about church history but this reverence for Antioch is an interesting relic of ancient times. The city still exists in Syria, but around the time of Christ it was the country's principal city and in importance ranked only behind Rome itself, Ephesus and Alexandria in the Empire. It is believed to be the first place in the world where the term `Christian` was used. This magnificent edifice dominates the square which is set amid a network of narrow roads packed with busy, expensive shops and tourists. They lead on to further smaller clearings where trees heavy with ripe oranges in April were a normal sight. It is of course tempting to follow the mandatory contempt for modern consumerism amid this ancient beauty and splendour. Only the other day I heard the hyperactive, arch-conspiracy theorist, Professor Noam Chomsky, lamenting the damage markets had done to society. Even a slight acquaintance with Liguria's history reveals that until modern times they barely had respite from invasions by French, Sardinians, more French, Saracens, more French, some Austrians and the French again. Personally I'd rather enjoy my coffee in the Italian sunshine watching tourists buying snow popes and alabaster crucifixes than witnessing important parts of people being cut off within reach of my espresso. I confess to being vulgar but I like markets. They encourage people to welcome foreigners, not to disembowel them. I shall be much happier when certain troubled areas of the world give up dying for honour, martyrdom, glory and traditional values and take up vulgar modern consumerism. I had experienced a city without markets in the old Soviet Union where Moscow was the dreariest capital I had ever encountered, almost as dreary as the prose style of the estimable but rambling Chomsky.

We then took a little boat round the coast to Portofino. This is said to be the most expensive and exclusive harbour and resort town in Italy. The harbour is famous. It is narrow but well sheltered on each side by steeply rising wooded hills, so I imagine it offered very effective safety for shipping. Again it had yachts but fewer than elsewhere. They also looked every bit as expensive as the ones in Monaco, but did look as if they occasionally went out to sea. No cars are allowed in Portofino, hence the boat trip. I gather you can drive to just outside it and then come in on foot or by donkey. Pliny the elder mentions the town and says the origin of the name is Portus Delphini or Port of Dolphins, apparently because of the large number of these creatures to be seen in the wider sea area of the Tigullian Gulf. The harbour itself is quite a site. There is a fine beach with buildings in the familiar ochre colour seen throughout Italy. Nowadays the beach is lined with restaurants under the shade of wide awnings.

Robert Noble Graham

Our party leader suggested that the best place to eat was one just a few yards across the sand from the jetty where we disembarked. I went along with the others and had a look at the menu. I could have had paninis with cheese, ham or salad, pizzas with eccentric combinations or focaccia with an equally wide range of fillings. Focaccia is native to Liguria and is widely available. It`s made from dough which is quite similar to that used for pizza, but with more leavening. That enables it to absorb large quantities of olive oil or, in some parts of Liguria, lard. The name is thought to come from the Latin *panis focus*, meaning `bread baked on the hearth`. The term is normally used to refer to `salt focaccia` which is the savoury bread. There is also a sweet version used for cakes.  Some of my companions settled down to what they told each other was `healthy Mediterranean cuisine.` I wandered off along the beach and came to a line of small eating places, each with a short menu outside. This suggested to me they were perhaps cooking very fresh produce. I went into one, wondering whether the famously opulent citizenry of the little town would disqualify me from serious attention. Not so. A serious, round-faced waiter wearing an apron welcomed me. His dark hair was carefully combed back and set with some very effective gel. His round face was matched with a similarly round body. I noticed with his first words that he had a surprisingly musical and resonant voice. Perhaps he was a great Italian tenor who had simply fallen on hard times. Modern opera is cruel and in our very visual age demands that its stars not only sound like someone you would abandon family and country for but look it too. I could not imagine my waiter climbing the ivy on tall buildings to leap dramatically into bedrooms, nor carrying a swooning heroine to his waiting horse, especially if the said heroine were on the same diet as he. Focaccia was not the food of heroes, I felt. He could probably have served up an excellent grilled dorada, but I am not aware of any opera plot that requires this valuable skill.

He brought me the menu. It was similar to the one outside except it was more precise. Instead of *pesce del giorno* (fish of the day) it had *branzino*, sea-bass. The starter was anchovies in ceviche, and the sea-bass was cooked in a lemon sauce. I am not especially fond of the strong flavour of anchovies but I knew it was a specialty of the area so I decided to try it. I felt it was likely that if anything would reconcile me to anchovies this place would.

I knew that Liguria produced some notable wines, many of which you can`t find elsewhere. They are often consumed entirely within Liguria and neighbouring regions. I asked the waiter if he could bring me a small carafe of something local that he would recommend. He nodded soberly, giving every impression of taking the request seriously although I was quite resigned to the possibility that he would simply bring me some of whatever was open in the kitchen. In fact he brought one made from the Vermentino grape which is rare outside of this region. It was one of the wines from the *Cinque terre* which is said to be magical but we would not have time to see on this trip. He explained to me that it was one from the region referred to by classical authors such as Pliny as `hills of the moon`. This, I gather, was a stamp of quality.

I resisted the wine until the anchovies arrived. I had tried making ceviche at home with onions, garlic, herbs and vinegar but had not been overly impressed with the result of quite a lot of work. This one did impress me and seemed to lend mildness to the anchovies which I appreciated. The wine was cool and delicious by contrast. The sea-bass that followed was accompanied by a few potatoes and two types of beans, all in a lemon sauce that had clearly also benefitted from a handful of local basil. It too was exquisite. No one else had come in yet so I decided to make use of the waiter`s local knowledge. I knew that one of the most famous sights of Portofino was one that most visitors never sea. I didn`t intend to see it myself. It is one of the oddest great sights anywhere. It is a statue of Christ under the sea. It is known as "Christ of the Abyss". The waiter smiled a little as if it was not the first time he had been asked about it and his reply had the air of having been rehearsed several thousand times. He told me it was sculpted by Guido Galletti in 1954 and placed at a depth of 17 metres. The figure has arms outstretched as a sign of peace. It is intended to protect fishermen and divers. My waiter had no opinion on whether it was effective in this aim. No, he had never ventured to see it himself. I had the impression he was happier to talk about Vermentino wine.

My lunch induced a languidness which threatened to obliterate the afternoon. I rejoined the others who had not necessarily enjoyed their paninis very much but did like Portofino. As a penance I decided I would walk up to the church that overlooks the bay. One of our company, Charlotte, joined me and the steep climb was well rewarded with the type of view over Portofino harbour that produces gasps in a cinema crowd. We were so enchanted by it that we almost missed the boat back, prompting suspicions in our group that it was not the view that had detained us.

Our next adventure was another coach trip along the coast. This time we were heading for Cervo. I had never heard of Cervo before this trip to Liguria. I don`t think many people have. It impressed me immensely and I would very happily pay it another visit. As we left our coach and looked up at the 16th century towers sixty metres above the blue sea beside the shingle beach we loved the place. It had apparently begun in the time of imperial Rome as the site of a large hilltop mansion for Julia Augusta. Around it grew a village largely devoted to coral fishing. Unfortunately it was our lot to have our first experience of the town in heavy rain. Since it was almost lunchtime by the time we reached it our guide led us from the seaside into a network of narrow, ancient alleys which rose gradually upward. We were walking on cobbles which were a little treacherous when wet. Our guide had given us no hint of how far we would be climbing so some of the older or more rotund members of our group became anxious and needed help to carry the cheeses and souvenirs they had rashly bought at our coffee stop in Imperia. Their gasps of relief were heartrending as we stopped to admire the increasingly spectacular view down the coast, the groans almost audible as we resumed the climb.

Eventually we reached a wide terrace which led to the very fine baroque church of San Giovanni Battista, also known as the *corallina* since it was where the populace in former times gathered to give thanks for the coral that brought some prosperity to the fishermen and the town. If you stood with your back to the church the view down to the beach and along the coast to San Bartolomeo al Mare was ample compensation to most of us for the effort. I noticed that one side of the terrace was Via Sandor Vegh. I was surprised to see the name of the great Hungarian violinist so far from his native country, although I knew he had left it at some stage. I learned later that he had founded a music festival here in 1962. It had evidently continued and flourished with him in attendance until his death in 1997 at the age of 75. He and fellow musicians had benefitted from the confusion reigning in Eastern Europe in 1946 to get out of Hungary and escape to France. He was particularly known as a great chamber musician and increasingly enjoyed giving master classes. I've often thought that making music with others of a similar ability must be one of the greatest experiences in life. He seems to have enjoyed that to the full. I have always loved music but my lack of talent is so extraordinary as to be worthy of scientific investigation. I felt the terrace in front of the handsome church, overlooking the blue sea of the Riviera di Ponente was a wonderful setting. Concerts there on a warm summer evening would have been priceless.

Alarm struck the hearts of our less mobile members when we discovered there was still more climbing to do. This took us a very short way to the top of the town and the restaurant where we would have lunch. It was the Locanda Bellavista, very appropriately named for perhaps the most beautifully located eating place I have ever been in. There we finally came to rest. A typically, smiling, relaxed and chatty Italian waitress exchanged gossip with our guide and then happily took our orders for several bottles of local white wine. She brought us one made with the Pigato grape which, like Vermentino, is native to this area. Some guzzled it with more eagerness than others but I think it met with general acclaim. I chose one of my favourite Italian antipasti *melanzane alla parmeggiana,* stuffed aubergine with parmesan cheese, followed by a seafood risotto.

On our final day in Liguria we went further along the coast to another of these picturesque towns by the sea. This one was Alassio where four of us found an excellent restaurant on a wide, sunny beach and had little trouble deciding how we`d spend our time if we were rich enough.

I have visited many places where a week was fully long enough to appreciate its joys, but a week in Liguria hardly lets you scratch the surface. A beautiful and interesting area.

THE COMPANY IN VENICE

Anyone who loves films will have seen quite a lot of Venice without needing a passport. The canals, the gondoliers, the bridges and the little alleys have been an irresistible backdrop in several Bond films, in comedies like "Blame it on the Bellhop" or "Indiana Jones and the Last Crusade", in literary ones such as "The Wings of the Dove" based on the Henry James novel or in very frightening ones like "Don`t Look Now" based on Daphne Du Maurier`s novel. People of my generation might associate it more with the cult classic "Death in Venice", based on the Thomas Mann novella. Not as frightening as "Don`t Look Now" but disturbing in its way. Depending on which films you`ve seen you may think it is either the loveliest city on earth or the most spooky. Music lovers know Offenbach`s very tuneful Barcarolle and one of Chopin`s greatest piano pieces is also a Barcarolle where you can easily imagine yourself coming down the Grand Canal at sunset and into the lagoon. So, it`s a city that can inspire people or unsettle them..

Robert Noble Graham

You don't really go to Venice to be on your own. Literary and artistic phantoms will certainly be all around you even if you avoid the hordes of tourists. I took my first trip there well aware that I'd encounter the two multi-purpose world wanderers of literature. Is there a bar in Europe in which Hemingway did not drink or engage in a brawl, either under his own steam or at the urging of his myopic, pugnacious but under-sized Irish friend James Joyce? "Deal with him Hemingway," resounded through the bars of Europe when the little fellow had managed to enrage yet another Frenchman or Italian. Is there a cliff – face in Europe from which Byron did not dangle or a turbulent maelstrom he did not swim to exorcise world-weariness? Does anyone recall they both wrote stuff worth reading? Well, I knew I'd come across them but wasn't really expecting the close company of others.

Henry James was another who haunted the city frequently. He remarked that he thought it impossible that anyone could ever say anything new about it. That may be true and might just make my current efforts pointless, but since very few readers will have absorbed everything ever said about Venice I'll continue. If I'm plagiarising someone I haven't read then we'll just have to accept that. At times it seems that James' life consisted of endless dinner parties anyway. He seemed to know people everywhere. By contrast, on my first visit to Venice I went without a companion but never felt entirely alone as I'll explain. That was not the result of the countless tourists. It's perfectly possible to feel alone surrounded by hordes of fellow creatures. However, I don't have Henry James' social circle either so the company was a little different.

I didn't go to the unique city with any literary aims in mind. I love Italy for its variety, its magnificent cities, its landscape, its food, its wonderful Italianness. But phantoms were awaiting me, and how interesting they were. I had been late in booking this trip for early March some years ago and there was no accommodation at acceptable prices in Venice itself so, fatefully, I accepted the travel agent's suggestion to stay on the island known as the Lido in the lagoon. Erudite readers may already sense what was in store for me. The Lido is quite a populous little island with shops, restaurants and hotels of its own. A twenty minute trip by water taxi will take you to Riva degli Schiavone where you come ashore to the unimaginable beauty of Venice.

Almost everything about Venice is hard to believe. The approach to it alone is unlike that to any other place I have ever visited. I arrived at the airport from which a water taxi awaits to take you to your destination. You step in and all around are the waters of the lagoon, the broad natural inlet from the Gulf of Venice, protected by the narrow necks of land known as littorale. I looked around in vain to see any sign of the legendary home of Titian, Tintoretto and the empire that had ruled the Mediterranean. The crossing of the lagoon on the map had looked so short that I had expected it to be not much more than a long paddle. But as the water taxi got under way no buildings were in view. We set off on this great ocean, as it seemed, as if saying goodbye to reality. That sensation grew as in the distance I saw the first towers of San Marco, Santa Maria della Salute and The Campanile rise hazily, shimmeringly, from the water. They looked insubstantial, unsteady mirages rather than buildings of stone. Gradually more detail appeared as if Titian were painting it in as we approached. Eventually, within sight of the landing by the Doge`s Palace it almost resembled a city in which people could live, but far more ornate, colourful and imaginative than any real settlement. It was quite late and I wanted to check into my hotel but first I took one stroll past the Doge`s Palace into Piazza San Marco, St. Mark`s Square, to see the renowned basilica. In the broad square in front of it were the expected crowds of pigeons and on the far side the long line of porticoes leading to shops selling every item of fashionable living. The Basilica San Marco itself is so dreamlike that the sense of the unreal that had come over me on the lagoon appeared to be confirmed. Set in a great western city it speaks of the orient as do spices and perfumes or the poetry of Omar Khayyam or the music of Scheherezade.

That, of course, is appropriate since St. Mark, the city's patron saint, was from the Middle East. Legend has it that he replaced the original patron, St. Theodore, when in 832 Venetian sailors brought the Apostle's bones from Alexandria in Egypt. The great empire once ruled from The Doge's Palace beside the Basilica stretched far into the Levant where the navy of this small city could deter even the might of Turkey under the sultans. Needing some reassurance that at least my hotel room was a reality I took another vaporetto to the Lido where reality was in plentiful, maybe even excessive, supply. My room was huge with two functional beds that looked more like army surplus than art nouveau. There was no bedding when I went in. There was a mattress on each, both of which looked as if children had used them as trampoline practice and one appeared to have been chewed by some creature. I was not wholly convinced the creature was not now inside it, bedding down to start a family. The porter appeared to visibly stagger when I told him I thought this was a dump and wanted a better room. His mind was suddenly wiped clean of the moderate command of English he had shown and he resorted to Italian exclamations with hand gestures which suggested that any tether he had ever had had reached its end long ago. Tasks such as finding another room in this fairly small hotel could not be expected of him. I suspected he was in line for a substantial bonus if he could persuade anyone to occupy this slum. I went down to reception where the perfectly pleasant young woman appeared to be fully ready for my request. In fact, there were rooms in the adjoining hotel which was also owned by the management and within seconds she gave me another room key, assuring me that the porter would bring my luggage. I found my way round to it and thought it quite acceptable. My luggage quickly followed, delivered by the same porter who now greeted me with smiles and a return of his mastery of English, entirely restored by his expectation of a tip which did not materialise.

On my first morning I walked down by the sea, turned right through the small town and reached the vaporetto landing. I was soon aboard and heading back to Venice, amused to see teenagers texting to their friends sitting a couple of metres away on the far side of the boat. A tall, lean, aging dandy who might have been expected to behave more sedately was tapping just as eagerly at his mobile phone, evidently delighted by the response. Was it an assignation with a lover, probably male, or had he just been confirmed as performing at La Fenice, the famous opera house? Probably something less momentous. No doubt all of these travelling companions were too familiar with this trip to share with me the thrill of that crossing, seeing the Doge`s Palace, the dome of San Marco and Santa Maria della Salute all coming into focus.

On coming ashore I simply walked without much purpose other than to admire everything I saw. The excited crowds of all ages, the romantically decaying buildings and the evidence everywhere of style and design were enough. Soon I was standing on a bridge looking down at the Grand Canal which opens into the lagoon. The bridge led on to an open market and suddenly I remembered "Signor Antonio, many a time and oft in the Rialto you have rated me."Shakespeare`s *The Merchant of Venice* had been a standard part of school curriculum when I was young. I imagine that has changed. Of course I had come from the Rialto bridge over the Grand Canal and I was entering the market where Shylock had regularly suffered the merchant`s abuse. Shakespeare, as always, had posed problems. Shylock was not always a very nice person on the evidence of the play. However, the treatment he got from the gentile citizens did not give him much chance to be nice or to feel loved. He had no choice but to be an outcast and that feeling distorts anyone`s outlook. Jews in significant numbers would have been relatively recent arrivals in Venice at the time that Shakespeare wrote. They were expelled from Spain in thousands in 1492 when their scholar, Nahamides, had, in the Girona debate, argued all too convincingly for Judaism against the Catholic scholars. Given four months to leave they ended up in many parts of Africa and Europe, some more welcoming than others. Venice, shrewd and mercantile, welcomed them for their contacts and commercial acumen, but had no interest in making them feel seriously at home. They were confined to an enclave or *gheto*, providing later Europe with a word of many chilling associations.

I watched the barges coming up the Grand Canal laden with fresh fish and fruit to be sold in the market. I walked by the stalls and saw women in headscarves buying for the family, and stylish couples hand in hand perhaps buying for a moonlit dinner in an apartment in Dorsoduoro. There seemed something strange about carrying out these tasks of everyday life in surroundings so spectacular. It was strange but it was reassuring. This of course was the city of Titian and Tintoretto, but it was not a museum. It was no longer the great mercantile and military power it had been in the time of these painters or, no doubt, of Signor Antonio, but it was now one of the enduring wonders of civilisation and a place where ,amid, the treasures, people bought food, cooked, loved and enjoyed the greatest of treasures, life itself. Standing on that renowned bridge with the Grand Canal before me, the laden barges passing and excited tourists bustling around me, I considered how pleasant it would be to return one day and take an apartment with a suitable companion and choose from the variety of tempting food on the stalls: fruit, vegetables of all colours and types, fish, meat, wine, cheese and flowers to adorn the dinner

Coffee, Chianti and Caravaggio

table. Then hurry back along the narrow alleys and over the little bridges of minor canals and, on a warm summer evening, have candlelit dinner on a balcony above the water where gondolas would pass. I believe, sadly, that on a summer evening the smell is likely to detract more than a little from the romance of such an idea.

I decided I needed coffee and perhaps something to eat. I had left the Lido quite early and breakfast had been light. I walked back a little way from the crowds, and just across from the casino where Wagner had once lived there was a café that was not very crowded at all. In fact there were no other customers. It consisted of three round tables with high stools at them and a counter behind which a man of around forty was reading a newspaper. He looked up from his reading and the absence of a smile was almost audible. There was the slightest jerk of his head as if to say "what do you want"? I looked at the range of food on display and none of it appealed. However, I was hungry, so I ordered a coffee and a pale looking sandwich. I thought of so many cafés in so many other parts of Italy where the delicacies would have been irresistible. Not here. I began to feel less surprised that there were no other customers. The man said nothing but pointed to a table and disappeared. I sat and read a guidebook. After a few moments I heard a brief "oy". A coffee sat on the counter and it was not going to be brought to me. I fetched it. Moments later I heard another "oy" which signalled the arrival of the sandwich which appeared to me to have sagged further in the few minutes since my order. It was clearly more embarrassed than was the proprietor by its own inadequacy. I consumed this tawdry repast quickly, feeling as if the dark little café were just a waiting room for limbo. Then I paid the man the requested sum. He looked outraged, evidently because I offered him no bonus payment for the extraordinary service I had experienced. As I approached the door he addressed me again in an angry tone. He wanted me to bring my dishes over from the table to save him the trouble. "Sorry, I don`t speak Italian," I lied, despite having ordered in that language. I suspected he was hoping to audition for the part of Charon, ferrying the dead to hell in some tourist –ridden travesty of Italian cuisine and charging for it.

I came out into bright sunshine more amused than annoyed. I briefly longed to go back in and ask what had soured his mood or, if he was always like that, why on earth had he chosen an occupation where it helps to be nice to people. However, these thoughts were swept away as I turned a corner back to the Grand Canal. The contrast with the gloom of the shabby little café was a revelation, like that magnificent scene in Beethoven`s Fidelio when the prisoners come out to the light. Perhaps it was also this sudden opening of my mind to light and beauty that made me think of Proust. How was it possible that the great Marcel had been disappointed by Venice? How could the man who could be made ecstatic by a cake not love these sumptuous views? I suspect the answer lay in his having conditioned himself by far too much reading of Ruskin's "Stones of Venice". Ruskin, the brilliant, infinitely knowledgeable English critic, possibly the `morning star` of environmentalism, had written from the point of view of a perceptive architect and artist. However, he totally lacked Proust's visionary capacity to see the world through the heightened, erotic sensibilities of a lover. Ruskin often gives the impression that he can only see Venice as a museum, a relic of past glories, even if a very beautiful one. Maybe all he could see were stones and not the gondolas mooring at the bricole or the light on the water as the Grand Canal passed Santa Maria della Salute on the way to the lagoon. To be fair to the great novelist he got over his disappointment quite quickly and wrote in *Albertine Disparue:* *'When I went to Venice I found that my dream had become – incredibly, but quite simply – my address!'* Like Wagner, Dickens, Balzac, Truman Capote and Salman Rushdie, he stayed at the Hotel Danielli. It would appear that staying there guaranteed worldwide fame. I have not stayed in it.

I went back round by San Marco cathedral and the Doge's palace to the Riva degli Schiavone. I walked past the Bridge of Sighs to a line of restaurants, all with merry young waiters trying to entice customers with broad smiles. I chose the one whose smile looked the least forced and ordered a pizza with a glass of wine from the Veneto. I sensed my waiter was disappointed I had not gone for the antipasti, prima piatti, secondo piatti, postre, espresso and bottle or two of Barolo. The pizza was no better than quite good and when I paid again I faced outrage from the cameriero whose dazzling smile had entirely gone to be replaced by a threatening scowl. This time I had paid the full bill plus service charge plus what I thought was a reasonable extra for what Italian waiters expect on top of the service charge. I shrugged. I was paying no more. I felt a kinship with Shylock. I felt he was lucky that he was only rated in the Rialto. I was getting it everywhere. Perhaps they felt Scotsmen and Jewish moneylenders were all of the same breed. I walked round away from the main thoroughfares past some more modern ,unpretentious housing, well away from great churches and monuments to western culture and came to the water again at what I realised was the Arsenale. This had once been the dockyard and harbour for the mightiest navy on earth, sufficient to subdue even the formidable Turkish fleet. This was where the ships set sail that Othello would have commanded on Cyprus before his tragic downfall. Now it looked empty and wistful, a lonely old lady remembering the times when she had no shortage of vigorous young men for company.

Coffee, Chianti and Caravaggio

I was a little tired now from the breathtaking scenes on the one hand and the rudeness which was so unlike the Italy I knew, as was the indifferent food. I decided to take the water taxi back and spend the evening on the Lido. There, I found a friendly, acceptable restaurant and turned in early. The short walk back from the town with the Gulf of Venice to my right in the darkness was surprisingly restful after the crowds of the day.

The next day I took the vaporetto early and reached the landing by the Doge`s Palace before it was excessively crowded. I took more time now to walk round to and into Basilica di San Marco. Again the immediate effect was surprise at how different this was from the Italian cathedrals I had seen in other great cities. Of course the onion dome effect of the exterior prepares you for this venture into an eastern world of icons and gold. This basilica was constructed in 976 after the first St. Mark`s was burnt down. It was a very clear reminder that in those days Christian Venice looked east to the church in Constantinople, now Istanbul, not to Rome, the western Christian centre. The Seljuk Turks had not yet taken Constantinople as an Islamic conquest. High on the façade, above the main entrance are the replicas of the four bronze horses which are a symbol of the city`s power. They were brought from Constantinople in the Fourth Crusade in 1204, having been constructed several centuries before, whether in Greece or in Rome is not known. The Arch-Pilferer, Napoleon, had them taken off to Paris to undermine Venetian influence, but they were returned under Austrian stewardship. The originals are now in the Marciano Museum in the basilica.

The interior of St.Mark's is a journey to an alien but immensely beautiful world of dignified saints and angels in wide ornate panels inlaid with gold leaf and studded with jewels. I found the central nave dazzling with its domed ceiling in coppery gold with icons all the way up to the high windows where the light enters. On the floor is intricate mosaic laid out in the form of a Greek cross. The language of the basilica is Greek, the original language of the Gospels, not the Latin of the Roman church. This was the chapel of the doges of Venice who ruled the Adriatic and beyond with power and style (the word `doge` is simply Venetian dialect for `duce, meaning a leader, effectively the same as our word `duke`). Today you can visit the Venetian harbour in a Greek island like Rhodes and admire the elegance and taste of what was left. That may well encourage you to feel that if you had to choose a foreign power to invade and overcome you the Venetians would be among the better choices. In the Baptistery, set out in colourful, carefully chosen mosaic is *The Dance of Salome*, a scene I have not found in any other church. Altogether you felt, going through this marvellous building, that its founders were much more relaxed about sensual matters than most of their neurotic counterparts in other religious outlets who often seem interested in nothing but sexual misbehaviour , as they see it.

The following morning I decided not to hurry into Venice. It was a pleasant morning and I opted for a walk down the road by the sea. I passed the town and walked beside tired looking guest houses and hotels until I reached one impressive looking one. Even so, it had a dated appearance and was no longer at its best. The name struck me. Hotel des Bains. I wheeled round and there behind me was the beach. Of course. I knew where I was. This was where Gustav Von Aschenbach had stayed in the tormented, complex *"Death in Venice"*, by Thomas Mann. The story was made into an art film by Visconti, starring Dirk Bogarde as the ailing, tormented, unfulfilled composer, sick with love for the Polish boy,Tadzio. Whether he was tormented with homosexual lust or haunted by this image of healthy youth in his decaying twilight years is not clear. Perhaps Mann himself did not know. Like his protagonist, Mann had stayed there with his family, not alone like his character, but doubtless feeling he was. He too, like Aschenbach, had seen a young Polish boy at the hotel and he too had fallen in love with the boy. The Venice of his story is not a glorious city but a cholera-ridden hell of corruption. Just as Shylock had felt an outcast in the Rialto so did Mann four centuries later, not because he was Jewish which he was not, but because he was secretly homosexual and indeed pederastic in its etymological sense of lusting after children. Then I thought again of Proust who had been both Jewish and homosexual and had written in *Sodome et Gomorrhe* of how similar was their story of exclusion, Jews and homosexuals. Both, as Proust argues, had contributed immensely to the society of many cultures and both had been oppressed and persecuted.   Sad that none of them had chosen what he was. All of them suffered for it.

I took the water taxi at lunchtime. I was intrigued by a couple of English women sitting across from me. They were chatting merrily, obviously loving Venice. What took my attention was that one was knitting what looked like a large sweater and never looked up either at her friend or the scenery as she did so. I didn`t like to ask if the skyline of Venice would be in the pattern. Nonetheless, they seemed to have a full programme of events ahead of them. They referred several times to one place they wanted to see. I couldn`t make out what they were saying for a time until I realised they were using an unusual pronunciation of Guggenheim. That reminded me that the Peggy Guggenheim Gallery was a recommended sight. I thought it would be an interesting change from the traditional style of the Accademia which, as great art galleries go, is a very good one, but I had seen a lot by this time. I left the vaporetto at the landing just beside the Doge`s Palace and walked across the Piazza San Marco. I don`t know how many times I would have to do that before I`d view it as an everyday event. This is particularly true on days such as this one when even the pigeons in the square must have felt outnumbered by the tourists. I don`t know if the original designers of the great basilica were really concerned about the professed Christian aim of bringing people together but if so they would feel now they had succeeded beyond their wildest dreams. I pushed my way through crowds of Germans, Americans, Scandinavians of some sort, various orientals and I don`t know how many subdivisions. I`m sure this was not an abnormal day for this great cultural landmark. I don`t think these people were united by any body of doctrine professed by the tenth century church fathers. I think they were united, as they are in many parts of the world, by sheer admiration of creativity. The same impulse takes hordes to the pyramids in Egypt, the Palace of Versailles in France, the Acropolis in Athens, Ankor Wat in Cambodia.

I went round by the opera house, La Fenice and past the Palazzo Barbaro to the Ponte dell`Accademia, the last bridge on the Grand Canal before it opens out onto the lagoon. The canal was busy with a number of gondoliers nonchalantly avoiding vaporetti, charging purposefully in either direction. Once across, if you go a little to the right you reach the Accademia, full of the great Venetian painters` works. If you go left you duck under an arch, across a little square and reach the splendid modern building of the Peggy Guggenheim gallery. I had ignorantly assumed that Peggy or Marguerite, her proper name, was simply the bored wife of one of the rich Guggenheims who had nothing better to do than buy countless works of art, some much better than others. I was quite wrong. If anything her life is more interesting than her gallery. She was not the wife of a Guggenheim. She was the granddaughter of Solomon R. Guggenheim who created the wealthy Guggenheim foundation. Solomon had inherited valuable mining assets and added to the family fortune with the Yukon Gold Company. She was the daughter of Benjamin who, for some reason, ended up with less money than his siblings. However, all things are comparative and a relatively poor Guggenheim is likely to be quite comfortable. Benjamin appears to have been born under an unlucky star since he drowned when the Titanic sank in 1912. Peggy`s inheritance was in the region of $2.5 million, which probably equates to around $34million nowadays, so she could always afford a bowl of soup. She was, however, far from idle. From her early days she was an ardent collector. It has been said that what she collected most assiduously in her life was men since she had countless affairs, reportedly having slept with around 1,000 before her death in 1979 at the age of 81. I am always sceptical of such figures. Who checks these numbers? That would, after all, be 25 men a year for 40 years which seems like a vigorous rate of activity.

There is no doubt that she made friends with many of the legendary figures of the avant-garde such as Marcel Duchamp, Jean Cocteau and Samuel Beckett, with whom she apparently did have an affair, and Max Ernst whom she married and quite soon divorced. She came early under the influence of the renowned English art critic Herbert Read and her gallery in London was largely filled by a shopping list of Read's recommendations. Apparently she is a character in the film *Pollock* made in 2002 by the very fine American actor Ed Harris. She was, I gather, largely responsible for launching Jackson Pollock's career. Her gallery is now administered by the Guggenheim Foundation set up by her grandfather.

The building itself is airy, modern and full of light. If you walk through it you come out at the Grand Canal itself so its setting could hardly be better. The exhibition is large and very varied. Many of the exhibits are clearly great creations. To my taste many are not and I couldn't help wondering whether down-at-heel artists simply rummaged in their backyard for junk they could persuade Peggy to buy. This is perhaps unfair but it was difficult to see the merit in some of them. I had strolled through to the Nasher sculpture yard which is a very pleasant way to view such exhibits in the open air amongst greenery and had looked round the museum. Both in the yard and the museum I was struck by the extent to which many of the works seemed to be enhanced by appearing beside others equally modern. I found myself enjoying many which, out of that context, I may simply have found odd and uninteresting. I reflected on this as I walked through to the terrace beside the Grand Canal and then back through the building to the café. There I fell into conversation with an urbane, distinguished –looking American gentleman who was evidently on his third trip to Venice since retiring as vice-president of an academic publishing company. The café was quite full and he had suggested I could take a seat at his table since there weren`t many elsewhere. We talked about the gallery and I confessed my reservations about some of the exhibits. He chuckled and sympathised with my puzzlement. He had wrestled with the same dilemma each time he had come. Had Peggy simply been more perceptive than we were or was she easily taken in by plausible looking young men with junk to sell? How would we ever know?

My week drew to a close and I had mixed feelings. Like so much of Italy a visit to Venice felt just like dusting the top of an immense treasure chest whose contents would take lifetimes to appreciate and understand. I had seen a lot of the visual arts for which it was justly famous but I had wanted also to spend some time finding out more about the great composer Antonio Vivaldi, the red priest, who had flourished there and had written some of the most loved music ever written, but there was no more time. I had walked past the legendary Harry`s bar, renowned only because it was yet another place where Hemingway had regularly drunk and brawled. I didn`t see any point in going in. That side of the great Ernest is the least interesting to me anyway. I had felt some of the bleakness of Thomas Mann as I had looked at the forlorn Hotel des Bains and had even had a tiny taste of the unmerited hostility which had surrounded Shylock, but certainly not to a degree that impaired my visit at all. It`s a small city but opens to a universe.  I was aware of John Ruskin`s amazingly learned and scholarly analyses of the city, the ones that had such a profound influence on Marcel Proust and many others. Perhaps because Ruskin`s whole way of approaching a city like Venice is so different from my own I have not been able to go back and read him in detail as I felt I should. I am really more worldly and entertained reflections that, I am sure, never occurred to the lofty Ruskin. I had also greatly enjoyed the writings of others like Jan Morris or Peter Ackroyd. I suppose the travel writer who has given me most pleasure on the subject is H.V. Morton. I think his appreciation of the place would have been more in tune with my own.

  My thoughts went back again and again to the notion of taking an apartment with a suitable companion, shopping at the market, sharing great meals with wine and very gradually unearthing more and more of the city`s treasures. Perhaps it will happen, but, unique as it is, Venice is just one amongst so many great sights the world

Robert Noble Graham

has to offer. I had, of course, felt company for much of the way, but great and legendary as many of these companions were they were no substitute for the living, responsive one whose presence I would hope to enjoy in that prospective visit.

DIVINE COMEDY IN FLORENCE

I had no thought of Niccoló Machiavelli when I invited my friend, Audrey, to join me for a week in Florence and Siena. I had of course seen them both before during my Tuscany trip with my son, Malcolm, but that had only left me with the desire to spend much more time there. The invitation could not, in any way, be considered "Machiavellian", and yet the shadow of that apparently unremarkable fifteenth century functionary of a minor Italian state colours all of modern Italy.

Florence began as a Roman camp and its name arose from the Latin *Fluentia* as the place where two rivers flowed. It lay on the main route between Rome and the North and had the advantage of also being a very fertile area. Like so much of Italy it was fought over by the Ostrogoths and the Byzantines, which did no favours for the population. Nor did the later Black Death which was virulent. Charlemagne in the 8th century followed later by Margrave Hugo chose it as a regional capital and its population grew rapidly to a number of something like 90,000 before the Great Plague of which more than a quarter are reckoned to have worked in the wool trade. There followed a struggle between the families of the Albizzi from Arezzo and the Medici. The Medici were themselves talented and resourceful but it appears that the remarkable astuteness, some might say deviousness, of Macchiavelli as their secretary and counsellor is thought to have played a major part in their flourishing. Macchiavelli understood perhaps better than anyone at the time that power lay not so much in having a mighty army as in having a network of useful alliances built up through the interdependence of trade.

Towards the end of the fifteenth century it seemed that all of Italy would be swallowed up by the great power and ambition of Gian Galeazzo Visconti, Duke of Milan. He had already subdued much of the country from Piedmont south. Venice was still mighty and could easily afford to turn its back on Milan`s ambitions, but it was not clear who else could withstand his power. The country was still shaking from the enormous battle between the Guelphs and the Ghibellines, supporters respectively of the Papacy and the Empire. The Guelphs had won, but had no sense of security. Gian Galeazzo gave Florence an ultimatum to concede but Florence refused. Florence had pursued a rather different course from its neighbours. It had become a city of merchants and bankers, especially under the control of the Medici family, reaching a peak with Lorenzo the Magnificent. Lorenzo had even survived the hostility of Pope Julius II in the famous and absurd Pazzi conspiracy. Gian Galeazzo marched with his immense forces on the recalcitrant city, but, embarrassingly, dropped dead on the way. The Florentines took this as confirmation that they had been right to embrace their mercantile lifestyle which promoted solidarity and cooperation as well as wealth. It also confirmed them in their admiration of classical models rather than those of either Christianity or the dark ages.

I had booked accommodation at Soggiorno Michelangelo. It was a rather unusual hotel set in Via Fra Bartolomeo. It was just outside the main centre but that merely involved a pleasant walk of about 15 minutes to reach the old city. It was a little unusual in that it constituted one floor of an impressive period building. It had seven large rooms, each with en suite facilities. In addition, it had a large reception area where a varied buffet breakfast was spread out every morning. The proprietor, Oscar, was a tall, lean man. We had a taste of his very individual approach when he professed deep disappointment on seeing us. We wondered why. He told us he had guaranteed all the other guests that Scots were arriving in Highland Dress, prepared to play the bagpipes. Audrey said we had regrettably had to leave our Highland Dress at the laundry and I pointed out that a blast on the bagpipes would probably empty his hotel rapidly and perhaps have us all arrested for breach of the peace. He grudgingly accepted this explanation. He then began to describe the facilities in Italian. I began translating for Audrey whereupon he halted with a look of alarm. "Am I to understand that the Signora does not speak Italian?" he asked. We had to concede that this was the case. He wrung his hands. "Che pena! (what a pity). Such a beautiful lady and she does not speak Italian." Audrey was quite untroubled by this eccentric behaviour and she assured him she would learn it very quickly. He nodded sagely, thoughtfully, the look of concern never leaving his face. Then he turned to her and said. "Of course, you do realise that breakfast can only be available to those who speak our language fluently."

"Oh hell," lamented Audrey. "I might be a bit late for breakfast then."

He smiled, not quite reassuringly, and showed us to our suite. The room was very large with a heavy wooden double bed against the left wall, a desk and chair under the window facing us, a leather sofa to the right beside the door and a sizeable TV opposite that. It was late afternoon so we decided to walk out in the sunshine and have a first look at the city. We turned left on leaving the grand building. The street itself was impressive. It was not tourist Florence, but these were obviously apartments of people who had means and taste, perhaps town residences for owners of estates large or small in the Tuscan countryside. We crossed the broad Viale Giacomo Matteotti and took Via Alfonso Larmarmoro which went past the Botanic Garden and some of the University buildings. The street then changed its name several times but led us directly to the Piazza del Duomo (the square of the cathedral.) This is the heart of the city and it is a magnificent one. Beside it is the Piazza di San Giovanni. This area is mediaeval and is probably not very different from how it looked to the young Dante, greatest of Italian poets, who was born around here in 1261. Having said that, the Duomo was not begun until he was an old man, nor was the Baptistry with its magnificent bronze doors. We walked past Michelangelo's enormous David, not the original which is in the Galleria dell'Accademia, but a very impressive copy. It is something of an irony that David, who won fame for being the small but heroic figure who slew the giant Goliath, should himself be immense, and yet it seems quite appropriate for his heroic stature. The sculpture of course had and has a special meaning for the Florentines, symbolising how it had stood against the might of Milan and Gian Galeazzo Visconti.

    A little further down we approached a café with seating outside, in view of the David and of the Uffizi Gallery. We sat down and a brisk, efficient waiter brought us two of the most expensive glasses of ordinary red wine we had ever enjoyed, but enjoy them we did. We fully accepted we were paying for the privilege of sitting in that unique area. The sun shone warmly on the red stone of the buildings and tourists wandered past, entranced as

Robert Noble Graham

we already were by the treasures around them. I think it was William Faulkner who said in *Requiem for a Nun* "The Past is not dead. It`s not even Past". Italy, like much of Spain and most of Greece illustrates this truth very well. Florence was famously and savagely torn between the Guelphs and the Ghibellines in the 13th century, between the Papacy and temporal power. Here, although we were in a city with some of the greatest religious buildings in the world, you are surrounded by very human achievement. In Rome the supreme triumph of the papacy is evident, making use of great artists for its purposes. Here in Florence the opposite seemed to be the case. Michelangelo`s David used a Biblical story but the real message was the triumph of the City. The Uffizi Gallery has many great religious paintings, but some of its most memorable works ,like Caravaggio`s Bacchus and Titian`s Venus of Urbino, have pagan subjects. The Popes ruled Rome, but commercial figures such as Lorenzo de Medici of the great banking family dominated in Florence.

We walked back since Oscar had recommended to us a restaurant near to the hotel. We thought it would be very nice after dinner only to have a short stroll to face. Light was fading as we got back to the Via Fra Bartolomeo and we were pleased with our decision. The restaurant really was only a few doors from Soggiorno Michelangelo. When we entered the youngish woman who greeted us achieved what, to my mind, should be the first aim of a good eating place. She made us feel welcome. That point seems so obvious I cannot understand why it is not evident to all restaurateurs. Off hand, I cannot recall having any complaint on this score in Spain, Greece or the United States. In Italy only on my first trip to Venice did I feel unwelcome in a couple of establishments. I may say that experience was not repeated on further visits. Some other countries which pride themselves on their cuisine do not seem to take the same view.

Audrey bravely decided to have her first ever taste of wild boar. This is sometimes on the menu in the U.K. but it is sometimes no more than feral pig. In Italy, like Spain, wild boar is still native. I chose a rabbit stew. Although the U.K. has an almost endless supply of rabbit they don`t often appear on a menu. British sentimentality about certain types of fluffy creature discourages it. Audrey was impressed with her choice. The meat was succulent and had that slightly more `gamey` quality that distinguishes it from domestic pig. It was so tender we assumed it had been marinated in wine, garlic and, we thought, cinnamon. My rabbit stew was equally satisfactory but it did seem to me I had been provided with the Arnold Schwarzenegger of the bunny tribe. The legs looked as if they had come from Bengal tigers rather than a rabbit. I wondered if there was some special crossbreed of rabbit with mammoth perfected in Italy but kept secret.

Robert Noble Graham

The following day was beautifully Italian with a warm sun smiling out of a deep blue sky. The ochre buildings of the city looked warm and friendly. However, before we could venture out we had to deal with Oscar`s condition that only fluent Italian speakers could have breakfast. I tutored Audrey to say "Durante la notte ho imparato tutta la lingua Italiana, ma sfortunato oggi l`ho dimenticata," which was my best attempt at the Italian for "during the night I learned the entire Italian language, but unfortunately today I have forgotten it." The genial Oscar smiled in appreciation and allowed that `accidents do happen` and he had found the British peculiarly prone to forgetting the entire Italian language.

I think we both felt a marvellous sense of freedom and excitement at going out to explore the great city. We took the same route as on the previous evening because it was evident that would surround us with great sights and experiences. We had been discussing this independence which Florence had managed to establish from the power of Piedmont to the North and from Rome. We were headed for the Duomo, a triumph of Italian architecture and art but also the scene of much of its history. One of the most telling but farcical incidents was the outcome of the Pazzi conspiracy. I have mentioned that much of Florence`s wealth and power derived from its role as a major centre of banking. That could give immense influence but also brought great dangers. One of the reasons Jews have been persecuted and exiled in European countries is a result of exactly this. Kings and other powerful people often ran up huge debts as they financed wars and coups. So, what do you do if you are a powerful but impoverished king or lord who owes lots of money to a banker, by no means all of whom were Jewish? If you can get away with it you kill them or expel them. Then they cannot collect the debt.

The mediaeval and Renaissance Popes were regularly short of money and they often turned for their financing to Florence, especially under the rule of the Medicis whose fortune had been built up over several generations. When Lorenzo the Magnificent was head of the family and business the Medici bank was only one of eighty in Florence, but it did have branches in 16 European capitals. Lorenzo himself was a highly intelligent and accomplished man. The terra-cotta bust of him by Andrea Verocchio shows someone both manly and humane. He looks the type of man who, as his biographer Machiavelli reports, had the strength and compassion to protect the poor from unjustified tax rises despite the hostility of rich and powerful Florentines.

The Pope at this time was Sixtus IV, one of the most active and creative in restoring Rome after the Great Schism in which a Pope sat in Avignon in France. He built the Sistine Chapel and greatly improved the Trevi Fountain.

However, he had one of the common papal weaknesses. As H.V. Morton observes: "The length to which aged bachelors would go in order to establish their ambiguous nephews in palaces is a curious psychological study." Sixtus wasn`t by any means the only Pope to suffer from this. He wanted to borrow a substantial amount from the Medici bank to set up his nephew in land neighbouring Florence itself. Lorenzo did not want any relative of the Pope so near at hand and refused the money. Sixtus responded by closing his account and opening one with the rival Pazzi bank in Rome. Francesco Pazzi not only stored up money. He also stored grievances and he felt he had plenty against the Medici. The Italian word for `stupid` is `pazzo`. That`s why in American gangster films the fall-guy is `the patsy`. Francesco, it seems, was well named. He decided it would be a fun idea to have Lorenzo and his brother murdered at High Mass in the Duomo. At times it can seem as if Renaissance Italy was overrun with accomplished assassins. In Christopher Marlowe`s play, Edward II, when the conspirators are having difficulty in killing the imprisoned king they hire an Italian who, by definition, would be an expert. Pazzi hired a number of priests including the Archbishop of Pisa. The one soldier he approached who might have been able to do the deed soon pulled out, perhaps out of scruples but quite possibly out of contempt for his proposed team-mates. The whole plan misfired, although Lorenzo`s brother was killed in the scuffle in which Pazzi managed to stab himself. Lorenzo had little difficulty in avoiding attack and recruiting friends to protect him. The hapless, witless conspirators then fled to the nearby Palazzo Vecchio. Not having done their research properly they did not know that the old palace had been fitted with a self-locking device so that when they went in to escape detection they could not get back out. They had considerately imprisoned themselves for Lorenzo to deal with as he pleased.

I have discussed the Duomo in the chapter on Tuscany when I first saw this remarkable building. Audrey was not yet accustomed to Italian churches and found the sheer extent of colour and imagery dazzling. I think I was at least as stunned by my second visit to it as my first. I had assumed that my memory had embellished the effect, but if anything I was amazed all over again. I was particularly taken this time by the intricate marble pavement, inlaid with unbelievable artistry in the 16th century and still a wonder. That led up to the marble sanctuary from the same period. Marble is not a substance you often find in British ecclesiastical buildings but it always seems to me to give a unique effect of both permanence and purity. It did seem a particular travesty that the farce of the Pazzi conspiracy should have been set there. We shared the thought that it was not easy to decide whether such a building was a monument to wealth and power or to artistic magnificence and spiritual striving. All of it seemed to be contained there. Of course, again we found it mandatory to climb the steps of the 85 metre high Campanile which stands beside the dome and from which the views over the city are splendid.

Mandatory also was morning coffee outside in the same expensive café where we had enjoyed wine on the previous evening in the Piazza della Signoria. Audrey is the type of person who has only to sit at a table in public to find a soul-mate. I had been looking at a guide book to work out a sensible approach to the endless treasures of the Uffizi only dimly aware of Audrey in conversation. Audrey drew my attention and I looked up to see a stout woman at the next table. She was perhaps fifty years old or a little more. What immediately struck me about this lady was that she was sweating profusely and yet wore a thick coat with, obviously a woollen jumper beneath it. I looked up. "Would you mind beginning that again Eileen?" said Audrey. "This is fascinating." Eileen who was also gulping steaming hot tea obliged. She spoke vigorously with a strong Lancashire accent. Eileen had evidently been a nurse but had in recent years been more involved in lecturing. This didn`t surprise me as she began a torrent of information in a voice very suitable to keeping listeners wide awake for a long time. However, I too was soon interested. Eileen had little concern for Michelangelo, the Medicis or even Florentine ice cream.

She was a kind of pilgrim to the shrine of Florence Nightingale who had, we learned, been born nearby. Hence her name. Her sister had been born in Parthenopolis in Naples, resulting in her middle name being Parthenope. Eileen felt indignant that the world knew so little about her idol. As she lectured on in the Italian sun, sweating disturbingly, we began to agree with her. Apparently Florence's arrival in the Turkish hospital used by the British in the Crimean war soon resulted in a dramatic increase in the nursing attendance and a dramatic fall of 90% in the weekly death toll. Not only that, but back home she had founded the world's first nursing school at St. Thomas's Hospital, and taught the woman who would return to the USA to do the same there. Evidently she was also a gifted mathematician who used statistical methods little known at the time. Pie charts were a familiar tool to her. She was also able to get things done in high places. At her instigation the great Isambard Kingdom Brunel designed a prefabricated hospital to be taken out to the Crimea to offer better working conditions. Eileen recited all of this (and much more) with hardly a pause. Then she did pause, looked at us and then admitted that what really interested her was that the great nurse's drive had come from a series of mystical experiences she had, Joan of Arc-like, calling her to the work she did. Apparently the first of them had come upon her when looking at the great Egyptian ruins in Thebes. During her lifetime she said very little about these experiences, but, Eileen told us, she had left some very interesting writings describing them. This did sound like captivating stuff and we both were momentarily tempted to tag along with Eileen. However, by the time we spoke she was almost done with the city. She wanted to visit Thebes in Egypt where `the spirit had spoken` to Florence and see if she could detect something herself. Then she wanted to find the hospital in Turkey where Florence had worked. I did find it interesting that Florence`s mystical experiences do not appear to have been in any particularly religious context. She was nominally a Christian, although a heterodox one. She appears to have believed that her own religion was by no means the only route to spiritual knowledge and had little time for sectarian views. Her influence on many aspects of British public health was extensive and profound and it seems that nursing standards in the hospitals of the American Civil War had been raised dramatically as a result of her. Eileen downed the last mouthful of her tea, wished us well and then, still sweating like a championship boxer and dressed like an Arctic explorer, she sped off in the general direction of Egypt.

The sun was now warm in the wide, busy square and we could understand why Michelangelo`s David felt much more comfortable naked, and with a physique like his he could be satisfied that the attention he got was all admiration or at least envy. He was also too heavy to be carted off by the police for indecency, which his status as a timeless work of art precluded anyway. We decided now to launch a modest assault on the Uffizi. From where we were sitting in the Piazza della Signoria we could look to our right down the Piazzale degli Uffizi. This is a broad avenue liberally spattered with pavement artists drawing children as proud or occasionally impatient parents looked on. Some people despise this activity as having nothing to do with art in the august presence of the great art gallery, but I admire what they do. Discussions of what is and is not art are, I think, entirely pointless. I usually find these drawings impressive and often very charming. I'd certainly rather hang one of these on my wall than half a dead sheep or an unmade bed which, evidently, the true art connoisseur prizes much more highly.

Of course, sitting where we were we really did not need to move to have a feast of culture. We could see the majestic series of porticoes along the ground floor of the Uffizi and the almost uninterrupted wall of glass which forms the upper story, created by Buontalenti, made possible by the iron framework demanded by his predecessor, the great Giorgio Vasari. However, nearer to us, immediately to our right, was the Loggia dei Lanzi, designed by Orcagna in 1382 to house the Lancers who were the bodyguards of Cosimo Medici I. Once when I was in business I had to visit Redford Barracks in Edinburgh

which lodged a unit of the British army. I remember turning up at the spare
gatehouse and being perused and questioned as if I had "Please note that I'm a foreign spy" tattooed on my forehead. After weighing the pros and cons of having me shot there and then the guard allowed me into the wide, empty yard with a couple of square functional buildings ahead of me. Even half a dead sheep and certainly a lady`s unmade bed, would have relieved the starkness of it. The 14th century Lancers of the Medicis had a much more picturesque dwelling. In the archway at its entrance are a couple of statues of anonymous Roman emperors, but nearer the front are two masterpieces. There are the arresting, struggling figures of The Rape of the Sabine Women by Giambologna, incredibly carved from a single bock of Carrara marble, and, a little further from us towards the corner of the Piazzale degli Uffici was the bronze Perseus of the great goldsmith Benvenuto Cellini. This statue from 1554 was intended as a warning to Cosimo`s enemies. The celebrated Greek hero, founder of the Mycenaean tribe, is holding aloft the head of the Gorgon Medusa, she of the coiffure of serpents. No one had previously been able to deal with this monstrous female since her gaze would turn you to stone. I had an English teacher like that once. We wondered why she always wore a hat. No one in his right mind would tackle Medusa, but Perseus, heroic but poor, had been

instructed by Polydectes that if he (Perseus) wanted to marry Danae (Polydectes` daughter) he would have to bring back the Gorgon`s head. Polydectes thought he had cleverly dealt with the young upstart, but Greek gods who were much more proactive in those days turned up unexpectedly and supplied Perseus with a ready-made Gorgon-disposal kit: winged sandals, a sickle and a burnished shield. He also got help from the Nymphs of the North but, to be brief, he caught the image of the Gorgon Medusa in his burnished shield acting like a mirror and was able to sever her head with his sickle. Then he flew off with his winged sandals before her ugly sisters (and she was no Cinderella herself) were able to intervene. We may find that heart-warming apart from members of the Hideous Gorgon Preservation Society whose views must be respected. However, the warning to Cosimo`s enemies was clear. You may think you are tough, but we can handle Gorgons. The threat would have carried more weight, as many would have known, in that the statue`s creator, the great metalworker, Cellini, admired throughout Europe, had, by that time, killed at least four men, one the Prince of Orange, and had been imprisoned (rightly or wrongly) for sexually assaulting several others.

However, our next destination was the Uffizi itself. We knew galleries by now and that a devil-may-care approach to them soon results in headaches, nausea and a worrying inability to find the way out. We had decided to look at some of the works of Duccio and Giotto to see how radical were the changes introduced by the latter to the wooden figures in earlier paintings. The change is quite striking if you see even the most distinguished of his precursors and then look at the *Ognissanti Madonna.* Life has been breathed into the canvas and you can see how that continued in the works of Ambrogio and Simone Martini. Our other aim was to move forward to one of the other great innovators of Italian painting: Michelangelo Mersi di Caravaggio. Caravaggio was only a name to me until I went to an exhibition of his work during my first visit to Rome. It involved a trek from the Church of Santa Maria del Popolo to the Galleria Doria-Pamphili and other locations. The use of light and shade, the sensuality, the audacity, the drama, sometimes blood-curdling, was so different from what I had seen before. In the Uffizi is his early painting *Bacchus*. This is probably a self-portrait of him as a teenager, then in the employ of a Roman cardinal whose interest in the good-looking young man may not have been wholly artistic. However, impoverished after leaving his village of Caravaggio near Milan, he needed a patron of some sort. Like Cellini, young Michelangelo Mersi, had a habit of getting into difficulties. He had a fight with Ranuccio Tomassoni which resulted in the latter's death. If you were going to kill anyone in Rome at that time (and lots of people did) Tomassoni was not the best choice. He came from a well-known family of the type best known to modern audiences from films like *The Godfather*. The term, *mafioso*, may not have existed at the time but the general set of principles certainly did. This began a fugitive life for the young man, taking him south to Sicily and eventually, strangely, to stay with Knights Templar in Malta. He appears to have been pursued by enemies for much of his life, and yet he continued to produce great masterpieces. He had a particular taste for depicting beheadings such as the tremendous painting of Judith and Holofernes in the *Galeria Naltionale d`Artica Antica* in Rome. This was a favourite theme of painters and sculptors down the ages. Donatello did a famous sculpture on the subject and even in the 20th century it was used with Stalin in the Holofernes role, finally decapitated in the triumph of ordinary people against tyranny. The original Hebrew story (in the Catholic old Testament but not the Hebrew one) tells of the attack by the Assyrian Holofernes on the city of Bethulia. Judith, a beautiful widow of the city goes to Holofernes` camp to appeal to him. However, she appeals to him in a rather different way and he invites her in. The original story is adamant that he did not molest her, preferring to drink himself stupid. Judith then took the obvious course of action to defend her city and decapitated him. Caravaggio`s painting shows Judith as attractive but not especially remorseful. The expression on her face is more that of a woman surprised at how easy it can be for an attractive woman to deal with a tyrant. Some see that as a fixation with castration but it seems to me much more likely that Caravaggio loved the idea of the weak, apparently powerless Judith, taking full revenge onthe figure of undisputed, arrogant power, Holofernes. I suspect he saw himself in the Judith role at least in his fantasies.

It's an interesting reflection on national stereotypes that nowadays we tend to see the Italians as a pleasure-loving people whose soldiers really did not want to be fighting in the Second World War. Their depiction in Louis de Berniere's novel, *Captain Corelli's Mandolin* reflects that view very well. However, as can be seen from the fight of Florence to remain independent and the careers of both Cellini and Caravaggio, violence was a major part of the country's history. In case anyone assumed that was only true of the distant past it is worth noting that in the post-war restlessness and rebellion of youth, very often student youth, the Italian left-wingers were by far the most violent and ruthless in western Europe. They produced, of course, the hideously bloodthirsty Red Brigade, but for a period it was not uncommon to hear of these mostly middle-class, affluent young `intellectuals` beating up figures of authority such as police or security guards who were normally from impoverished agrarian or other working-class backgrounds whom the Marxist-Leninist students claimed to support.

I think we judged our visit to the Uffizi quite well. We had found the chosen displays fascinating and enlightening and producing no more weariness than can be dispelled by a well-chosen ice cream. We headed down towards the River Arno which was not far away. The Arno is, I think, much more impressive than Rome`s Tiber, although it very much depends on when you see it. It is notoriously variable, running almost dry at times and at others causing very serious flooding. The flooding in itself can be bad enough but as Audrey and I leaned over the wall to admire the flow of the river up to the Ponte Vecchio we noticed a couple of very large and well-fed looking rats swimming near the far bank. Having hordes of these rodents tumbling out along with the floodwater would multiply the horror significantly.

We turned away and continued to stroll towards the Ponte Vecchio. We had hardly set out when Audrey spotted an ice-cream shop. It was more a palace than shop. Somehow its treasury of very perishable goods was suddenly more valuable than all the enduring marvels of the Renaissance. Even Caravaggio could hardly have matched the array of colours set out before us from blueberry, tangerine, vanilla and peach flavours. Then there was almond, chocolate, coffee, pistachio, pina colada, campari. "How is a girl supposed to choose?" complained Audrey. The only solution was to buy as many of the flavours as would fit in one giant cone and persuade me to do the same. Then, in a hot Tuscan day, we had the mighty task of consuming as much as possible of the rapidly melting wonders, exchanging cones with amazing rapidity to get some experience of eight of the exquisite options.

We soon reached the Ponte Vecchio. I expected Audrey would be fascinated by the line of ancient jewellery and souvenir shops that straddled the river. This is thought to be where the Romans built the first crossing of the river. It is the narrowest point. It has had major restorations and refurbishments since then, one supervised by Giorgio Vasari himself. One of his alleged innovations was to construct a corridor on the top by which Cosimo I could walk, unseen, from the Pitti Palace across the river to the Uffizi, thereby depriving himself of a visit to the ice-cream shop. Since its earliest times the bridge seems to have been a prime setting for merchants. As a result, it has given us our word `bankrupt`, *banca rotta* in Italian. The merchants would set out their wares on a table or *banca*. If they failed in business and were unable to pay their debts the wares were cleared from the table and the table physically broken or *rotta*.

The influence of the Medici family in Florence is pervasive and even if you are not impressed by sculpture, painting or architecture there is a fascination in seeing just how wealthy one family could become in the 13th to 15th centuries. We are currently disturbed by the wealth, deserved or otherwise, of bankers, but that is not a new phenomenon. We visited what had been the family`s parish church, San Lorenzo. It is situated in a Piazza of the same name which sits at the northern edge of the area which had been the old Roman forum. It says something for the influence of the Medici that their presence almost obliterated that of the great imperial power of classical times.

As with so much of Florence, like other Italian cities, a proper analysis of its wonders would take a large volume or perhaps several. Even one building such as this one is a study. The original dome of the church was designed by Brunelleschi but almost a century later work was done in it by Michelangelo. He submitted designs for the façade which were never implemented, but he did design the very individual staircase and the tombs in the Sagrestia Nuova. Michelangelo was of course one of the greatest and most original of all artists. However, if you look at the tomb of the Duke of Nemours you have to wonder if he ever really looked at a woman. The tomb has two gigantic figures representing night and day. The one on the left (`Night` I think) is supposed to be female. I know that he was thought to be homosexual and therefore had limited erotic interest in the female form. However, even when the Olympic Games showed us alleged females from the Eastern bloc remodelled (to put it kindly) by chemical substances they still managed to look a little more fetching than what Michelangelo sculpted. As I stood looking at it I imagined the great man saying to Leonardo Da Vinci (also allegedly homosexual but far better at drawing females) "Say Leo, what do women look like?" Leonardo might not have thought the question serious or perhaps saw this as his chance to show his great rival`s limitations. He might have answered: "Well, Mikey, just think of one of these hulking men you do. Subtract a few bits and add a few bits and you`ve got it." "Thanks Leo, you`re a pal. Thought I might actually have to go and look at one." After all, there were plenty of them around. He surely didn`t even have to go to the lengths of asking them to take their clothes off. Almost certainly he was already aware of the work of the great Venetian, Titian, who did some very convincing female nudes. Admittedly, he did a lot of them for the Emperor Charles V who appeared to see them as a modern might a copy of Playboy so perhaps he didn`t show them around. Private viewing only. Whatever the reason I find it hard to take most of Michelangelo`s females seriously as anything other than alternative men. Of course the one important exception I know of is the great Pietá in St. Peter`s in Rome. Mary, holding her crucified son on her lap, looks delicate, vulnerable, entirely feminine. It is not an erotic image and, of course is not meant to be, but that is a woman. I remain puzzled.

We came out to sunshine, a need for coffee and an antidote to cultural overload. A short walk took us to the Piazza della Republica which is largely surrounded by 19th century buildings. It also is lined with some of the best known cafés in the city. We chose one named *Giubbe Rosse*. Audrey asked if that name meant anything. I recalled the famous aria *Vesti la Giubba* from *I Pagliacci.* It means `on with the motley`, `motley` being the multi-coloured costume of a jester. I suggested it had to mean something like `red costumes`. "Sounds like we haven't escaped from culture after all," moaned Audrey good-naturedly. "This is Italy," I pointed out. The interior was a grand edifice with high ceilings and elegant archways from one room to the next. The bar was in polished dark wood with glass shelf upon shelf behind with endless wines, liqueurs, whiskies and brandies. Around the walls were paintings and drawings in a multitude of styles. On one wall there was a range of nudes, both male and female, all delicately done. "Michelangelo should have had his coffee here," suggested Audrey. We went back outside and sat in partial shade under the awning. A slim, dapper waiter appeared before us. He had a waxed moustache and his grey hair was carefully combed back. He introduced himself as Renaldo. We commented on the artwork. His eyes were already twinkling, more at my companion than at me, which suggested that his tastes were not those of Michelangelo. He explained that since the 19th century the café had been a centre of Italian cultural life. He claimed that `modernism` had begun there, whatever that meant. Even more recently, he maintained, it had been patronised by the Nobel Prize - winning poets Eugenio Montale and Quasimodo. Suspecting, no doubt, that this free helping of culture was not our priority he asked what we wanted. This produced some excellent coffee.

Whether it was the Italian sunshine or cultural atmosphere but we did feel a little of the `dolce vita` mood settling around us. We didn`t feel like doing anything much so we had lunch there after our coffee. Then we felt we had better move before someone mistook us for Bernini statues. We strolled languidly back past San Lorenzo to Piazza di Mercato Centrale which, as it sounds, is the location of a huge market, selling all kinds of fruit and vegetables along with wine, liqueurs, cheeses etc. The whole atmosphere was lively and colourful and soon dispelled our somnolent state. We smiled at the Italian habit of holding a conversation with someone on the far side of the Piazza rather than one close to you. We joined housewives pressing melons and looking thoughtful, hoping everyone believed we knew what we were doing. Gradually, we bought one tempting item after another, added a bottle of wine and decided to go back to our apartment for a little fiesta and siesta. Once ensconced we enjoyed the Bacchanalian evening and stayed in.

The following day we went to Siena as planned, but torrents of rain fell all day and we accomplished little. The day after was sunny and warm. We decided it was time to cross the Arno and visit the Pitti Palace. This enormous building was begun in 1458 by the merchant Luca Pitti, a friend of the Medicis. A century later Eleonora of Toledo who was the wife of Cosimo Medici bought the palace which was used to house many of the Medici treasures which remain today. Subsequently it was occupied for a time by the King of Italy and then by Napoleon. It never ceases to amaze me that tyrants like Napoleon, Hitler, Stalin etc thought they had a perfect right to take over the home of anyone, grand or humble when it suited their purpose. Today it is owned by the Italian state, but a group of volunteers known as "Amici di Palazzo Pitti" (Friends of the Pitti Palace) concern themselves with raising funds for its maintenance and arranging improvements.

The walk to the Palace from Soggiorno Michelangelo was around two miles, so a coffee stop was mandatory along with idle contemplation of Italians and some of the 5 milllion visitors who pour into the city each year. So, we reached the square, Piazza dei Pitti in time for an early lunch. The warm midday sun suggested that a seat at one of the outside tables was appealing. A waiter with a definite Robert de Niro look approached us promptly, wiping the table vigorously as he welcomed us. "Yes, I know I look like Robert de Niro," he began, hardly looking up from his polishing work and without our having yet mentioned this point. "And, certo, that`s who I am. Io Roberto de Niro, grande attore. What would the signora and signore like to drink. The right answer is vino de casa, our wonderful red wine. My name is Alberto."

"Not Roberto?"

"Non oggi. Not today. In disguise."

"I think I`ll have red wine," said Audrey. "And your disguise is rubbish."

Alberto, or perhaps Roberto, shrugged. "The beautiful women they all cruel. No?"

He left us menus and sped off to the kitchen. Two women, perhaps in early forties at the next table smiled at us.

"Did you get the same treatment?" asked Audrey.

"He told us Al Pacino but we didn`t buy that. He`s more De Niro."

"You American?" I asked, noting the accent.

"Shh, we're pretending we're Canadian. There's a bit of Ant-American hostility in Europe just now." This was shortly after the invasion of Iraq. I felt sorry for them. Whatever one's view of American Government action it was hardly their fault. After all, most Italians didn't want to be judged by Silvio Berlusconi's behaviour.

We looked across the square at the immense palace we intended to visit. It was large but, at first sight at least, lacked something of the style we expected in Italy.

"It's not the loveliest palace I've ever seen, I commented."

They smiled.

"It is a bit industrial," remarked one appropriately. You could imagine machinery and assembly lines in it. "It's pretty impressive inside and the gardens are lovely, especially on a day like today."

The two ladies turned out to be excellent company as we chatted to them over lunch. They both clearly worshipped George Bush Senior, father of the more controversial one then in power. They had apparently seen the former President a couple of times at events. "Tall and much more handsome in real life", they told us. We were in no position to dispute this.

After lunch we ventured on the immense building. It was like a microcosm of Italy itself in that you immediately feel unequal to the task of appreciating and assimilating it. It has 14 rooms of royal apartments, a Palatine gallery with 500 Renaissance paintings, a modern gallery, a costume gallery, a porcelain gallery, a silver museum, a carriages museum and then you stagger out to the beautiful Boboli gardens, designed for Eleonora of Toledo. Here, for the cultural marathon competitor are works by Michelangelo and Buontalenti as well as the magnificent *Venus Bathing* of Giambologna. A perpetual question in my mind as I go round such places is how much the patrons who invited such great works really appreciated them. Were their lives enormously enhanced each day as they gazed out at the work of the great Flemish master, Giambologna, while downing a breakfast of quails eggs washed down with Valpolicella? Or were they perhaps like some rich purchasers of Scottish castles I have known who rarely notice the spectacular views from their windows over mountain and loch as they consider what else to spend money on? I'll never know. Perhaps they were just spiritual giants in those days.

Florence is wonderful but we had a certain sense of relief on flying out of it. I became a little nostalgic for holidays in the Canary Isles where there are no palaces or great sculptures to see and you can give yourself over to sunshine and hedonism. On the journey back we agreed that the right way to deal with Florence is to have a cottage in the Tuscan countryside from which you could visit great cities, alternating with days of exploring villages and countryside, sampling local food with an occasional vintage. Not entirely unlike the first visit I had made to the country with my son. That acommodation was probably a little sparse but the ambience had been perfect.

Robert Noble Graham

BANQUET IN BOLOGNA

I used to live in a flat before I bought the cottage I now occupy. I was a little surprised one day to discover that I had a new neighbour who had chosen to move to Scotland from Lake Garda in Italy. Most Scots would feel that was a surprising decision, however patriotic they might be. The prospect of more and warmer sunshine than we normally get would be conclusive. However, despite its abundance of attractions Italy is not, I gather, always the easiest of countries to live in. Its bureaucracy can, apparently, be difficult, and getting things done can all too often depend too much on having the right connections rather than just cause. Probably no society is free of that, but my new neighbour, Jim, was not the only person to have told me it could make Italian life just too wearisome.

I got to know Jim reasonably well. He could be good company, but he did have some difficulty in not talking about himself endlessly. He had done some interesting things but there are times when even the most absorbing subject palls. He earned his living as a travel manager and his knowledge of foreign countries was encyclopaedic although it did lean a little towards the tastes and pastimes of middle-aged Europeans and Americans with large appetites and weak bladders. Jim himself did have taste whether in clothes, food, wine or opera, but sadly had all too rarely accompanied travellers who shared these interests.

One consequence of Jim`s lifestyle was that he had come across a large number of Italian caterers and vintners who had gifted him crates of quality wine. One evening he invited me and our other neighbour, Caroline, in for a meal. We had little idea what to expect. Could he cook or was the opportunity to talk about himself to a captive audience simply too great to resist? We arrived at his door. He was short and a little rotund but he had dressed like an Italian with a black shirt and trousers that both looked to be of high quality. He also wore a light waistcoat more for style than any added warmth it would supply. The smells of garlic, basil and wine- enhanced cuisine were welcoming. Caroline gave me a look as if to say the first impression was reassuring.

We went into his lounge. Books, CDs and photographs enhanced the Italian effect of the aromas. He entered with a white serviette over one arm. In his other hand he held a bottle.

"This is a light, dry, white from the Veneto," he began. "You`ll note a hint of lemon and grapefruit that makes the taste buds sit up and beg for great cooking." He began. "I asked them at Valvona and Crolla (Edinburgh's premier merchant of Italian food and wine) what they would charge. They were so eager to be put in touch with a supplier. They'd ask no less than £45.00 a bottle –no less."

Caroline and I had often shared a £6.00 bottle over lasagne so this was undiscovered territory for us. We had to agree this was a step- up in quality as well as expense. We felt the evening could be rewarding. We enjoyed the wine as Jim described how he had walked through these very vineyards only a few years before. Then we were summoned for the first course or `antipasto`. This was fettucini in garlic, cream and parmesan cheese. Our glasses were whisked away and he returned with others into which he poured a slightly more `forceful` wine from Emilia Romagna, slightly coloured by oak but `judiciously` controlled. We were advised that Valvona and Crolla would kill for supplies of this. I think we were both very surprised at just how flavoursome this starter was. The wine too was splendid although we would quite happily have stayed with the first bottle, but that was not an option. We were able to enjoy both food and wine undisturbed because Jim's monologue ensured there was no requirement for us to say anything. We just ate, drank and enjoyed. This time our glasses were topped up so we could `pause` before the `entremesa`. As we did so, it occurred to us that perhaps the reason Jim hadn`t let us finish the first bottle was that he was knocking it back in the kitchen as he worked. This impression perhaps grew a little as he summoned us for partridge and venison casserole which was brought in with a little more panache than we expected even from Jim. In no time he appeared again, his voice a little louder and his waistcoat a little askew, as were his vowels, as he explained:

"This, well, Dio Mio, Valvarolla and Crumpet or whatever they`re called. " He sloshed generous amounts of a dark red wine into yet more glasses. "This, well. What can I say?" (not very much, it now seemed, at least not entirely coherently). "Well, well I could tell you a story." He sat down and we realised there were tears in his eyes. "This is the wine of ……di queste sere cuando il mio cor." He choked. I explained to Caroline that this was the wine of these evenings when his heart did something. We assumed a woman was somehow involved in this story as a result of whom his heart either leapt or broke, we thought. Since both of us had now enjoyed a few glasses ourselves and had our own wounds from the arrows of cupid we sympathised. It wasn`t very clear to any of us what the others were getting tearful about but we were as one. Somehow we gathered that Valvona and Crolla would probably send out unpleasantly persuasive people if they suspected the priceless vintage we were enjoying.

`Enjoying` may be the wrong word since we were now slurping it without very much discrimination.

I think that even a little hazy as we were we appreciated that not only was the wine excellent but so was the casserole. It was a good evening. That needlessly long introduction is simply to explain why, when I was wondering which part of Italy to visit next, I consulted Jim. You will understand that I did this on a day and at a time when our alcohol levels were modest. I was surprised when he suggested Bologna. He gave his reasons. It`s not as tourist-ridden as better known places. It`s a beautiful city. The food is the best anywhere. It`s a good centre for visiting other marvellous cities like Modena and Ferrara. Its history goes back a long way with, possibly, the oldest university in Europe and its size is very manageable.

I was convinced, but because of the way life sometimes is it was years before I had the chance to follow Jim`s advice. Eventually I went with my friend Suzie who had done a lot of travelling outside of Europe but not much inside it and had never visited Italy. As usual, I went into the internet and found accommodation in a house near the centre. It was in via Massimo d`Azeglia. This is always a risk but there was a good website and I exchanged a few messages with the owner, Alfonso. That established that we could have a room with en-suite bathroom. Breakfast would be served in the lounge which we could also use at other times. Despite all this, it is a relief when you arrive if you find you have chosen well.

The physical appearance of Bologna is memorable, especially if you have seen other Italian cities. Rome and Florence can seem like the stages of a mighty tussle between architects, designers, potentates and Popes to build ever more astonishing churches and palaces. Bologna, whose historical centre is neatly contained within 12 ancient gates on a ring road, looks more like the work of a creative biscuit maker, operating on a grand scale. Most of the buildings share a terra cotta colour and the remarkable colonnades which go on and on from one street to another suggest a degree of mutual planning and organisation that is rare. It has numerous great churches and several impressive squares but none have quite the same sense of self-importance as you get from St. Peter`s in Rome or the Pitti Palace in Florence.

Our taxi dropped us at Via Massimo d`Azeglia. We approached the door to our apartment block and stopped to admire it. It was huge and wooden such as I have only seen in Italy. I should think it was at least fifteen feet high with heavy brass handles. The block itself was on three floors and simply formed part of the elegant, but understated building that ran from one corner of the street to the next, containing several individual addresses, some apartment blocks, some shops with perhaps offices or apartments above. As with so much of the city, a portico ran along it and we stood under it admiring the line of strong pillars on the wide pavement which supported the building, joined by sweeping arches. As the road gave way to the next one leading to the centre the colonnade continued , simply sweeping round the curve in the road but maintaining that remarkable sense of unity the city possessed.

We went through the door to an immense vestibule with a wide stairway and an old-fashioned lift of the type that has a trellis metal door which folds in on itself like an accordion as you open it and then stretches as you close it. We went up to the second floor and were welcomed by Alfonso. He was a man of middle height, aged perhaps 55. He had an amiable, well-meaning face with thin-rimmed spectacles. His slightly portly frame was adorned with a multi-coloured shirt, mostly yellow and red above dark trousers. He looked casual but definitely stylish. The shirt was noticeable but not gaudy. What unfortunately did catch the eye and slightly detracted from his fine appearance was his wig. Like so many hairpieces its colour was an impossibly uniform black but that might not have been so striking if it were not so obviously wrongly positioned. It appeared to be sliding off his head onto his right ear. We tried not to stare.

He showed us in and, just as we had been in Florence, we were amazed at how large an apartment in an Italian city can be. There was a short hallway which led into a spacious lounge. Its walls were papered in blue with large floral motifs. There was a carpet which, like the upholstery of the two generous sofas and four chairs, had a modern, abstract design that was understated, leaving wide areas between the small, leaf-like patterning. The ceiling was high and the room bright since there were two 12 foot windows which overlooked the street on our right. On our left was a French window which clearly led to a small balcony. The whole atmosphere was of taste, comfort and refined brightness. Immediately to our right on entering was a small kitchen. Alfonso led us diagonally across the room to a door. It opened onto a passageway. Our room was straight ahead of us. To the right the passageway led to other rooms. Our suite was also spacious and furnished with the same taste and, we assumed, expense, as the lounge. We too had a French window which opened onto the same balcony as that from the lounge, but further round the building. The balcony looked onto an interior courtyard where plants in green, blue and yellow hung down from other properties and the paving below had plant pots with small trees. We were delighted with our choice.

Suzie didn`t speak Italian but, as a Brazilian, she was bilingual in English and Portuguese. Her knowledge of

Portuguese helped her to understand some Italian. I do speak Italian but it was useful that when I missed some of Alfonso`s rapid-fire conversation Suzie understood it. Once we had seen our room Alfonso offered us some coffee and a quick run-down of what was worth seeing in his native city, of which he was obviously fond and proud. He smiled broadly when we confirmed we knew of its reputation as the gastronomic capital of Italy. He immediately marked on his map the seven restaurants he liked best. Knowing little else we decided to follow his advice. This is perhaps not the best decision I have ever made. We had been told beforehand of the merits of the restaurant Al Pappagallo in Piazza della Mercanzia. Alfonso agreed, we thought a little reluctantly, that this was worth a visit. We were eager to sample this renowned cuisine.

Bologna has a number of claims to fame. It specialised in a type of sausage which became known simply by the name of the city. That sausage then entered the English language in another context as the word `boloney`, for anything of doubtful truth. It is also often cited as having the oldest university in Europe. This is probably true, but that accolade is not quite straightforward. Oxford certainly had university buildings long before Bologna as did Cambridge and Paris. The first university building in Bologna dates from the 16th century. However, a university is much more than buildings. It seems certain that groups of law students were gathering in Bologna and seeking out teachers before any similar activity was happening elsewhere in Europe. It was probably the first city with a methodical attempt to rescue learning from the dark ages. Its student population swelled quickly and this is perhaps the most convincing of the explanations for the extensive porticoes. The pressure on accommodation for this swollen population was so great that this solution was found. Buildings could add rooms upstairs above the pavements as long as they were supported by the endless sequence of pillars, permitting uninterrupted passage below. An ingenious and elegant solution. The University has had many famous students and teachers. Thomas á Beckett was a student there and Luigi Galvani a professor. The university is also notable for having had female professors as early as 1209. The celebrated writer Umberto Eco, author of *The Name of the Rose* is a more recent member of staff.

Suzie had paid more attention than I had to Alfonso`s urging that we should visit the Sanctuary of the Madonna di San Luca. I had simply gathered that this place was somewhere out of the city in the hills. I felt that possibly this had been one of the times when his precarious hairpiece had seemed most distracting to me. Anyway, we didn`t have a car and I thought the city would have enough to occupy us. As she recounted what Alfonso and the guidebook had said I became more interested, especially as the weather promised to be warm and sunny and perhaps churches and museums were not the best place to spend our time in these conditions. Evidently there was a walkway which made the 300 metre climb quite simple. We decided that would be our aim followed by a visit to *Al Pappagallo* in the evening. The name means `the way of the parrot` which was not necessarily an enticement but we did not dwell on that.

That resolved as a plan for the following day, we decided, as it was mid-afternoon, to walk out to the town and end up at one of the other recommended restaurants to sample its fare. We went out to a warm afternoon, taking advantage of the shade from the portico. There was something terribly welcoming about the biscuit colour of the buildings on either side and we discussed whether it recalled childhood stories of gingerbread houses. We had walked for less than a quarter of a mile when, on turning right, we saw across the road a wide, inviting square. On the right were the pillars of another long, deep portico. In its shade a young guitarist sat making extraordinary music with nimble fingers. There were tables where people lounged and chatted in the afternoon sun and beyond that was the statue of a slim gentleman with a wig which had been properly fitted, dressed in the long jacket, waistcoat and short leggings of an 18th century man of consequence. He appeared to be studious since he was absorbed in a book. He was Professor Luigi Galvani and the square bore his name. Galvani was a considerable scientist, perhaps best known for noting the reaction of dead frogs to electrical impulses. This led to a long debate with his near neighbour Alessandro Volta of Padua. Both brought great distinction to their universities and to Italy. Their names of course have survived with the process of galvanising and the volt as a unit of electricity. It is said that Galvani`s report on the effect of these impulses on dead frogs was part of the reading of Mary Shelley in the summer when she began writing her great work *Frankenstein*. As we admired the urbane gentleman on his pedestal I reflected that the creation of Professor Victor Frankenstein was destroyed by the ignorance and brutality of human beings unable to understand anything different. Poor Galvani`s life showed a similar tragedy. He refused to sign the oath of unquestioning obedience to the new Cisalpine Republic under French rule, another legacy of Napoleon, the mad Corsican. Every financial support was taken from him and he died in poverty and depression. Death by over-zealous bureaucracy is clearly not a new phenomenon in our tormented world. This was in 1798 and was a final blow for a man who had never really recovered from the loss of his wife in 1790.

We sat at one of the outdoor tables in the piazza in the warm afternoon sunshine. The air was still and it was like a mild sauna. The guitarist continued to play dazzlingly, showing no interest in collecting money, simply absorbed in arabesques of splendour. Possibly they were riffs. Despite my advanced age I only came across the word in the last few years in this context. Earlier I had taken it to be only the name of a tribe of desert Arabs celebrated in an old English musical called *The Desert Song*, based on one`s understanding of Arab culture if you have spent your life in Surbiton. In the musical context the word seems to be used exclusively by rock and jazz musicians. Therefore, it is probable that this young man could never be considered as having played a riff. I felt the knowledge was not essential to my enjoyment of Bologna.

The waitress was young, smiling, energetic. I struggled to place her accent although her English was very good. I guessed at Sicily. Suzie suggested she sounded more Irish. Suzie was correct. Our attention was drawn to a couple at a table a little closer to the porticoes and the musician. The man was silver-haired with dark glasses, a cigar and a white suit. The jacket was unbuttoned and his blue shirt, rakishly open at the neck, stretched over a waistline that owed more to the vineyard than the gymnasium. The woman was at least 25 years younger. She also wore dark glasses. Her skin was unblemished and her figure desirable. Her dark hair looked expensively coiffeured. They were chatting. She laughed readily and he smiled. They were comfortable with each other.

"Are they lovers or father and daughter?" I asked. "If lovers, why on earth is she with him?"

Suzie laughed.

"Why not boss and secretary?"

"They`re not very hard at work."

"I`d guess father and daughter."

"We`ll never know."

"He might be kind and charming."

"As well as rich, you mean?"

"Well, you don`t want a pauper, but kind and charming counts for a lot."

We talked a little about Galvani and considered that in this mild sauna of an afternoon, after our journey and enjoying a glass of wine, galvanised is what we were not.

"I`ve only ever known the word as meaning getting prodded into action," Suzie said. "I suppose it has a real scientific meaning."

I supposed that too and felt it might be something to do with electrical charges plating a terminal with metal of some kind, but how or why escaped me. We undertook to find out. I later discovered that indeed it meant covering ferrous metals with zinc to prevent rusting. It seemed unlikely that the popular term `galvanise` in the way Suzie had used it to mean 'being prodded into action` could come from this. In fact it almost certainly derives from the dead frog experiments whereby an electric charge seemed to bring the poor creature back to life. I only discovered all of that some time later. As we sat in the Bologna sunshine we remained unsure. Whilst pondering this yawning gap of ignorance our attention was taken by an older woman, elegant but sedate, arriving at the table of the older man and young woman. She kissed both and they shared a joke. Then she sat and the man summoned the waitress.

"Father and daughter," we agreed.

Our first evening ended a little disappointingly. We chose one of the restaurants on Alfonso`s list. Our only criterion was that it was the nearest to our lodgings. I`ll say no more about it than that we thought it a poor advert for the city`s cuisine.

The following morning we turned up in the luxurious lounge of our accommodation and found Alfonso had set out a colourful and tempting range of Italian pastries and breads for breakfast. Neither of us was accustomed to eating delicate almond croissants and marzipan slices so early in the day. However, we did enjoy the cheese and cold meats he also put out and his coffee was excellent. He was wearing a slightly different variation of brightly coloured shirt with dark trousers. What had not varied was his wig. I had never given much thought to hairpieces before but I found myself wondering whether one removes them at night as you might your make-up if you are a lady. If so, how come he constantly failed to position it properly? If he didn`t remove it why did it not move around to another inappropriate position on the pillow? Possibly that was the problem. At some stage maybe it had been attached with such powerful adhesive that it could never move again, condemning him to wander the cruel earth with a permanently dislodged wig.

My attention was brought back to current matters by Suzie asking me to reply to Alfonso`s question about why we had chosen Bologna. I gave a brief account of Jim`s remarkable meal for my neighbour and me. He showed a deft alertness to marketing opportunities by immediately handing me a couple of cards and asking me to pass them on to Jim.

Suzie and I then set out for the Sanctuary of the Madonna of San Luca, a simple walk which should take not much more than an hour, we were advised. We set off and made for the Porta Saragozza, an impressive mediaeval stone gateway. Just before we reached it we passed a large statue of a monk, looking a little more active and less sombre than such statues normally are. I was intrigued to see that it was a statue to Padre Pio, the renowned priest to whom so many paranormal events had been attributed. His true name was Francesco Forgone and he was born in the little town of Pietrelcina in Campania in 1887. Very early in his life he began to experience visions, ecstasies and the stigmata. Later, healing miracles, prophesies and even bilocation (being in two places at the same time) were attributed to him. The story goes that he took the confession of Karl Wojtyla whilst he was still a humble Polish priest. Pio prophesied that Wojtyla would reach the highest place in the Catholic Church, which of course he did as Pope John Paul II. Graham Greene, the great novelist, who spent most of his life as a catholic of a sort once went to Pio`s cell for spiritual guidance but turned back at the last minute, saying he was afraid because he had been told it was impossible to lie to Pio. Greene felt that lying was an indispensible part of the spiritual life. Italy is a country where the church is omnipresent and where churches are constantly full. It`s also a country which has more active belief in witchcraft and the supernatural than most. Padre Pio is, nonetheless, remarkable in all this in that so many stories have surrounded him, but I have no idea whether any of them are true.

We continued through the gate, across the ring road and on to the Via Saragozza, walking, inevitably in the shelter of a long portico. We passed cafés both humble and grand with tables on the pavement, shaded from the sun which was becoming very warm. Suddenly, we both came to a halt beside what ,to me ,is one of the true wonders of Italy, one of the greatest triumphs of civilisation. It was not a sculpture or an exhibition of Coreggio or Caravaggio. It was not an architectural wonder or a fine library. It was not another lavish church or monastery, Armani shop nor even a football stadium. What we had happened on was a *salumeria*. The nearest translation, I suppose, is `delicatessen`. This was a beautiful shop whose window and interior had lines of bottles of different shapes, colours and labels which contained wines, liqueurs, olive oil, vinegar, almond oil. There were soft white cheeses and harder, more yellow ones. There were blue ones, deeply veined with mould and creamy ones to spread. There were different sizes of loaves, round or long, dark or white. From the ceiling hung large hams and sausages like mortadella. Intriguingly, beside us as we stepped inside was an assembly of small and slightly larger barrels. On them were the words in Italian for `chestnut, oak, acacia, cherry, ash and mulberry`. We had no idea what these were. We would have to wait until later. We promised ourselves a return visit to this shop when we had time. Now we wanted to reach San Luca.

We continued along the portico until we noticed a sign across the road pointing to the Sanctuary of San Luca. We followed it. This seemed sensible but turned out not to be. It took us to a quiet but modern looking country road.

There were green fields on either side and it led sharply uphill. If we hadn`t known the Sanctuary was quite near we might have hesitated in the warm sunshine, since we had only brought a small bottle of water. For a climb of 300 metres, much of it in shade, we felt that was enough. The Sanctuary sits among trees on the Monte della Guardia, so-called apparently because that is where the soldiers were stationed who watched the rival city of Modena for hostile moves. We knew there was a restaurant beside the sanctuary. We admired the green fields we were passing and enjoyed the warm weather.

The summit of this climb was clearly not far off so we pressed on boldly. Unfortunately, when we got to that summit the road turned left, which we knew to be away from where the Sanctuary was situated. This was annoying and the sun was getting hot. However, another turning should do it. We continued. All the next bend did was make us wonder whether we should go back down. I noticed a bus stop with a timetable on it. I looked at it. "The bus does go to San Luca." I reported. "How often do they go", enquired Suzie. I looked carefully. "Twice a day. The next one`s in six hours." We trudged on in silence. I wondered if there would be a cool mountain stream, or even a tree offering shade or a bus back downhill. I kept all of these questions to myself. Suzie apologised to me for suggesting this trip. I apologised to her for not having understood the directions better. We had both understood that the road was shaded from the sun and was only 300 metres. We both quietly wondered why not a single bus, car, peasant on a bicycle or tractor had passed us. I wished I was in Scotland where no walk in the country is complete without a torrential downpour or a cool mountain stream or at least a truck belching reassuring diesel fumes, one that could be hailed or, at a pinch, hijacked. On we went in hot, unrelenting silence. I remembered Humphrey Bogart doing this in some film about the treasure of the Sierra Madre. I seemed to remember he shot his companion to save water, or perhaps that was another film. I tried to banish the thought and hope Suzie had not seen the film. Suddenly, she said "Look, what`s that?" There was a definite spire far to the right. "That must be it," I said. "This road has been taking us away from it." "What if that`s not it?" she worried. I looked at her red, hot face to see if she was serious. "If that`s not it then we ask for a drink of water and the quickest way back down to Bologna." There were times when Suzie could be argumentative, but this was not one of them. I think she was lost in admiration for my ability to sum up a situation. The road tantalisingly still led away from the glimpsed tower for a bit and we thought of perhaps just plunging across the nearest field in the general direction of the building we had spotted. I remembered Humphrey Bogart doing this and ending up in a quicksand. I told myself that for quicksand you need water of which there was clearly none here. There are times when an encyclopaedic knowledge of Hollywood cinema is not as helpful as one would want. Mercifully the road turned and the building grew and grew into a large, majestic, very Italian structure. Hoping it was no mirage we stumbled on, finally coming into the settlement. The Sanctuary is a large dome atop a circular church all in sober, brick -red coloured stone. A wide stairway leads up to the entrance, narrowing as it climbs. A curved wall comes round the building to each side of the staircase, like a pair of protective arms. I did feel that if one of the arms had been holding a cool beer that would have been perfect. That was the form in which `sanctuary` was taking shape in my mind.

We no doubt looked hot, tired and bedraggled and compared to everyone else we were. The place was full of visitors, but even the older, more out-of-condition ones looked cool and relaxed. Suzie drew my attention to others, similarly cool and relaxed, emerging from a path which, we soon discovered, was the walkway from Bologna, sheltered from all kinds of weather by a colonnade two miles long. Nor was that colonnade difficult to find. It was simply the continuation of the one which had taken us past the delicatessen and from which we had unwisely departed on seeing the sign to San Luca. We learned that this superb structure, begun in 1657, had been built gradually over a period of sixty years by private citizens and guilds. It had been constructed to enable pilgrims in all weathers to reach the sanctuary of the Madonna of Saint Luke, but the saint was also adept at recruiting attendant virgins, one of whom had the responsibility of looking after Bologna, but not, as we had discovered, of misguided travellers who cannot be bothered to listen properly to Alfonso`s directions. The other purpose of the colonnade was to ease the passage of this virgin when caring for the city. Saint Luke of course was a doctor but, bad as our condition was, our principle need was a seat in the shade, some cool drinks and nourishing Italian food. The restaurant on the hill, where we settled, was all the sanctuary we needed.

The church on the hill is very fine, with a Madonna which, encased largely in silver, shows distinct eastern elements, betraying its apparent origins in Constantinople. Also impressive is the view from the hill of the surrounding countryside of Emilia Romagna, the province of which Bologna is the capital. As you come out of the church you have added elevation, above what the hill offers. The sanctuary is surrounded by a variety of lush trees in varying shades of green. Amongst them the cypress trees which are such a pervasive feature of the Italian countryside spike upward. It can be hard to believe, looking out on this peaceful, supremely civilised scene that there was any need for a military presence, especially one to keep an eye on innocent-looking Modena. You can still see the Via Aemilia, constructed by the Romans in 187 BC to link Rimini with the Adriatic coast. Pilgrims would use it in ancient and more modern times, heading for Rome. Beside it the great cities of Ravenna, Ferrara, Parma and Modena grew up along with Bologna. The powerful families of the Malatestas, the d`Estes and the Bentivoglios all used it to impose their influence, pursuing intense and often savage rivalries that seem out of keeping with today`s peaceful scene. Rivalries continue but more restricted to football and perhaps gastronomy, although there they are also happy to cooperate with Parmesan cheese and ham, Balsamic vinegar from Modena , pancetta or coppa from Piacenza. Different types of pasta, a variety of fine wines and exquisite patisseries are shared amongst the towns. It is also noticeable that there are more pigs in Emilia Romagna than humans.

We were very happy to descend by the legendary colonnade with its blissful shade. We were also intrigued by the many tiles and little plaques which record the names of people or institutions which had contributed to this wonderful piece of civic cooperation.

We needed a rest and went back to the apartment. By evening we were restored and decided to visit *Al Pappagallo*. Its name ` the way of the parrot`, if slightly amended to `the way of the birdbrain`, was perhaps an appropriate, if humbling, summing up of our daytime trip. Mercifully, it was a short walk down again towards the town centre for a hundred metres or so, followed by a right turn along Via Barberia, past the Piazza Luigi Galvani where we had sat out the day before. Then a left turn into Via Castiglione and the restaurant was just off this in Piazza della Merchandise. This restaurant is almost a century old and its owners have chosen to maintain it as if it were a refuge from the present day, a step into a past where service was more sedate and quiet, where colours were subdued and where furnishings recalled the 1930s rather than today. We were welcomed by a smiling, slim gentleman in a dark suit who suggested a corner table to us but made it clear that we were free to choose elsewhere. We were happy with his suggestion. Each table was set for four people and had white tablecloths and each chair was of dark wood, upholstered for comfort. On each table was a lamp. Perhaps most strikingly, around the walls were dozens, probably hundreds, of old photographs of figures from Italian history of the past century. Most of them were unknown to us, but we spotted Gina Lollobrigida, Marcello Mastroianni, Alberto Moravia, Arturo Toscanini, Sophia Loren and a few more.

We had decided before arriving that we would share each of the courses to get the maximum pleasure from our visit, hoping it would impress us more than the rather ordinary and overpriced meal of our first evening. We both liked the sound of jellied chicken with pistachios and radiccio and also tortellini in capon broth, which we knew to be a local specialty. To follow we chose strigoli with green zucchini, mussels and squid and tournedos of beef with parmesan and tomato emulsion. Neither of us had ever tasted strigoli before and, as far as I know, this is the only part of the world where it`s relatively common. It`s a salad green or herb which tastes slightly bitter. To drink we had some of the Lambrusco which is native to the region. We waited in anticipation, feeling we had earned a treat after the turmoils of the climb to San Luca, but cautious since our first taste of Bologna`s cuisine had not been great. Lunch at the Sanctuary had not found us at our most discriminating so as yet we had no settled view on this subject. The restaurant was not busy and this made us feel that the service was very personal. We enjoyed our first taste of the wine and resisted the bread and bread sticks. We had been prepared to wait for each course. If this was quality cuisine then we accepted it might take some time. In fact the meal began relatively quickly and as bite followed bite we decided Al Pappagallo, and perhaps Bologna, deserved its reputation. The food was excellent and the atmosphere perfect.

The following day I alarmed Suzie by saying I felt we should visit the city`s gallery of modern art. It has the amusing acronym Mambo (Museo d`arte Municipale di

Bologna), suggesting Latin dance more than painting. We didn`t know each other very well at this stage but she knew that I could get interested in some peculiar things. I think she might have been less alarmed if I`d suggested a haunted graveyard at midnight. However, not wanting to appear difficult she came along, taking comfort from her knowledge that my caffeine requirement would probably put an end to proceedings quite soon, at least temporarily. Although the gallery was at the far side of the city centre it was on the ring road and a very convenient bus service went round it. We both rather enjoyed bus journeys when abroad. You feel much more part of the everyday life of the city than you do admiring another great Guercino or Correggio. The building that houses the gallery is quite interesting in itself. It`s a former bakery and its current role began in the late 1990s when Lorenzo Sassoli di Bianchi, then head of Italy`s leading health food company, *Vasoli,* became President of the Gallery of Modern Art. The Gallery had existed for decades but had outgrown the older premises. It is now an airy, modern, bright building, although the chimneys of the old bakery are still discernible on the ground floor.

The gallery does have some fine paintings by modern Italian artists like Bosco, Corsi Carlo or Francesco Franco, and for a brief time Suzie, who has a discriminating appreciation of good art, felt reassured. However, I quickly dispelled that by leading her upstairs to the ultramodern section. We entered another bright, clean, spacious room decked with a pile of torn cardboard in one corner, some twisted, rusting metalwork in another, what appeared to be a pile of assorted rags against one wall and a video, apparently of someone's intestines shortly after digesting a pizza, whether wood-fired or not was not explained, as the central exhibition.

Suzie looked at me with an expression of total bewilderment and said:

"Do you like this stuff?"

I smiled and replied:

"What I like is this."

I indicated one of the explanatory plaques that were attached to the wall beside each of these pieces. The one beside the pile of cardboard read something like (I confess this is not verbatim, but close):

"X(I won't name the creator) feels strongly that the matrix of disposibility informing modern existence, qua existence, disguises and yet at the same time strangely expresses the rage of western impotence. The morphic dismantling of this display boldly seizes the underlying disintegration for which the disinherited modern soul secretly yearns. The materials chosen are deliberately and designedly alienated from traditional graphic modalities."

Coffee, Chianti and Caravaggio

Suzie looked at me.

"What on earth does that mean?"

"My guess is it means the artists knew this was junk."

We both burst out laughing. Suzie had got the point.

"Let`s look at another."

We looked at the video plaque. It read:

"Signora Y rebels against the post-Renaissance and, still more, post-deconstructionist, urgency to reach out for signification in the transcendental and necessarily ephemeral noumena, *pace* Kant, as unknowable *Ding an Sich*. Signora Y is haunted by the call of interiority since only that endogenous correlation of corporeal with ethereal can offer existential *Dasein* in polyerotic fulfilment."

"Wow, she`s even better, isn`t she," said Suzie.

I agreed.

"It used to puzzle me that people went to art school for years and came out tearing cardboard. That takes no creativity. What does take imagination and probably years of training is the garbage they put on these plaques. At the same time, I do feel a certain kinship with Signora Y."

"How so?"

"Well, she`s haunted by the call of interiorality and I have to say, my tummy is telling me it`s time for coffee."

We sat with our coffees in a fine, airy café and Suzie said to me:

"Can I make a request if I promise not to take you up to San Luca?"

"Of course."

"I`d love to go back to that salumeria and find out what these barrels are all about."

That was easy to agree to. We spent some more time looking at some quite interesting paintings and then set off. We stopped for a light lunch which, again, was no better than all right. We then strolled again through the warm, biscuit-coloured town, past Padre Pio and the Porta di Saragozza and arrived at the wonderful shop. When we went in the owner, a cheerful, energetic man of around 35 was serving an elderly customer who seemed very uncertain of what he wanted and what he was able to afford. This gave us time to look again at the mysterious barrels which were mounted on the left as we entered. They sat on a large wooden structure about two metres high, consisting of two parallel strips of wood which stretched the whole height and were supported on four wooden legs. Then wooden shelves were placed at intervals up towards the ceiling. Each shelf held one or more barrels with the largest at the bottom and the medium and smaller ones higher up. In the rest of the shop several large hams hung from the ceiling as did various types of sausage such as mortadella. On a shelf behind the server and just below his head height were rows of jars of chutneys and relishes. Above that was another shelf with cold meats of various kinds and above that rows of bottles of olive oil, vinegar and wine. To the server's right there was a glass case with truckles and wedges of cheeses such as Parmeggiano and Sardo Pecorini along with Gorgonzola and Dolce Latte. Other shelves held more jars along with packets of herbs, flour and seasonings.

The young man finished with his elderly customer who, it seemed to us, had left with goods worth at least twice as much as he was asked to pay. Luigi, his name as we soon discovered, then turned his smiling attention to us. We complimented him on just how beautiful we thought his shop and he returned the compliment by saying how much he loved Scotland: the scenery, the golf, the whisky, the people. Then we came to our question. What was in these mysterious barrels. He laughed. "Cherry, acacia, chestnut, oak don't tell you the answer?" We shook our heads, entirely defeated. "They are the different stages of maturing of balsamic vinegar." This would never have occurred to us. Apparently the full maturing takes about 25 years and the final product costs more than most wine.

Robert Noble Graham

Of course we bought a small amount at some cost and treasured it. I have used it since coming back. With some dishes its quality is evident. With others, I have to say, the cheap version from supermarkets does the job quite well.

That evening we set off for another of Alfonso`s gastronomic recommendations. This one was a short walk away from the town centre where we had one of the most entertaining evenings of our trip. It was warm and there were tables on the pavement. A waiter was standing idly beside one. There were no other customers. He stared at us as if he couldn`t imagine why we had stopped. I told him we would like to eat. He almost looked offended as if we had turned up at a stranger`s house and had demanded food. He agreed to this, gave us a look of alarm and disappeared inside. Minutes later he emerged with another young man, this one red-haired. They both, at a guess, were in their late twenties. The red-haired one looked at us also as if uncertain what to do. I asked if they had a menu. Their expressions changed. That obviously struck them as an inspired suggestion. With some discussion they managed to find a couple of glasses of house wine and some water. The first waiter now appeared with a pad and a look of terror on his face. Suzie chose a starter and main course. On seeing a look of total puzzlement on his face I tried repeating the order in Italian. He appeared not to have heard of most of the food on the menu. He disappeared. We were left with the wine and some bread. Time passed during which each of the men briefly peeped out, apparently to see if we were still there. It was clear that something was terribly wrong with this restaurant. Had something happened to the owner and two distant relatives with no restaurant experience had found themselves in charge? Were they the victims of some family joke or student prank? We had no idea, but we decided we were not going to get any acceptable food there. We left them what we thought was enough money to cover the wine and left. No one seemed to notice. No one emerged to chase us down the street. Interestingly, no one else had entered the restaurant since our arrival. They knew something we did not.

It was still not late in the evening so we decided to stroll back in to the centre and perhaps find a reasonable eating place or even a café with acceptable snacks. It was warm and people were walking around unhurriedly, simply enjoying the weather and the town. We headed back along Via Massima d`Azeglio, past the Basilica of San Petronio and soon found ourselves in the main square, the Piazza Maggiore. We noticed there was some activity to our right, in one of the main streets that led from the square. We decided to explore and what a revelation was in store for us. As we approached we saw stall after stall ahead of us of food. Shops were also open. The first broad stall we came to was selling varieties of sausages, both hot and cold. Behind it was a brightly lit shop that was selling young capons turning on a spit, chicken breasts, wings and legs on trays, having been cooked in various sauces. We came back out to the street and the next stall had fresh courgettes and zucchinis, squashes, fennel, artichokes and aubergines. Then there was one selling roast peppers with olives and tomatoes, various types of pasta and potato salad. On we went, passing wonderful displays of cheeses, bread of various types, olive oils and balsamic vinegar, fruit, roast pork. Side streets had more displays with aromas that were captivating. People milled around, chatting, laughing, some eating, some interrogating stall owners delighted to explain and describe their wares. We decided we were grateful to the restaurant for having been so comically hopeless. Otherwise we might never have found this bonanza of temptations. We were now hungry. We bought chicken legs in garlic and pesto, marinated courgettes with peppers, pasta with olives, a small loaf of rough brown flour, two cheeses, one hard and one soft and some chocolate delicacies. Excited, we now hurried back to our apartment, trying to decide how we were going to eat all this. I remembered I had some paper plates I had brought for food on the plane journey and I had some plastic cutlery.

This turned into the best meal we had had in the city and at last we could fully understand its reputation.

Everything we tasted was superb, prompting us to go back and interrogate the suppliers about how they could make capons taste so succulent, what they had done to the quiche to make every mouthful a miracle. Clearly, any visitor to Bologna who has any interest in quality food should rent an apartment and buy the local produce. Bologna has many more restaurants than we had been able to sample and Al Pappagallo had been excellent so I don`t pretend to be an authority on its eating places, but our short experience certainly suggested the self-catering route would pay dividends. Just exploring more salumerias such as Luigi`s would be a joy in itself.

Walking around any Italian city is likely to produce surprises and delights. On one of our strolls we walked past the impressive old buildings of the music academy where, standing in the street and paying no money to anyone we were able to listen to a vigorous and passionate soprano giving a stirring rendition of *Casta Diva*. The great aria of the priestess on Bellini`s *Norma* became quite well-known to cinema goers who saw the film *Philadelphia* in which Tom Hanks gave a portrayal of a young AIDS victim. The performance gave him his first Hollywood Oscar. A little further on we saw a large, dark-varnished wooden door which was majestic even by Italian standards. It was slightly ajar and we peeped in. A notice informed us that this was The Spanish School. Entry seemed to be unrestricted so we quietly walked onto the stone floor of the vestibule and admired a cloistered square. The wonderfully serene and solemn entrance held a surprise in a small statue we noticed just beyond the cloistered yard. It turned out to be an image of Saint Clement. What was surprising and endearing was how much he differed from the normally sedate and aloof figures of saints. He was an elderly, bearded man standing with his right index finger to his mouth as if totally perplexed about how he had got there. It would have been good to know how this little figure had come about but we saw no one we could ask. The Spanish School, we learned, was the only survivor of the twelve national colleges into which the University of Bologna had been divided. The others had simply been absorbed into the main institution.

A little later we headed down Via Santo Stefano to the remarkable Abbazia di Santo Stefano. It stands in a wide, cobbled square, on the one side of which is the inevitable colonnade under which people sit at the tables of cafés and restaurants, enjoying shade from the warm sun. On the other is the large, brick-built mass of the Abbazia. This is, in fact, a collection of four churches, formerly seven. The oldest part is San Vitale e Agricola, dating from the fifth century, making it the oldest of the city`s many churches. It contains the relics of the saints Vitalis and Agricola who were martyred in the 4th century. I found it very thought-provoking to wander through this great mass of ecclesiastical building that had survived through the ages, recording penance, martyrdom and devotion, and then to cross the square to have our coffee amongst the crowds enjoying sunshine, leisure, companionship, food and drink. What immense journeys the human soul travels to find its needs. Of course, in the fifth century A.D. and perhaps even more so in the thirteenth century from which some of the other churches dated, at the height of the Black Death, life on earth was likely to be, as Thomas Hobbes in *Leviathan* famously said: "continual fear, and danger of violent death; and the life of man, solitary, poor, nasty, brutish, and short.". Hobbes was referring to the condition of man without good government. However, his dictum applies equally to one where no government is strong enough to resist invasion of armies or, infinitely worse, virulent disease. For many people, just to hold on to their sanity it was necessary to believe the real world was the spiritual one to come when there was no body to be attacked by plagues, pestilences or torturers. Now that we can simply cross the square in the Italian sunshine to have an excellent coffee or glass of Chianti it is hardly surprising that our focus has changed.

I wondered as I looked at the austere walls of the ancient church with the sarcophagi of the martyred saints just how differently I would have viewed life and death in these uncertain circumstances. I think of it whenever I hear comfortable people disparaging materialism or western democracy. Some of the great monuments of the past like the Abbazia should give them pause for thought if they genuinely try to understand how insecure were these conditions. It further astonishes me that people can hold these views when it is not so long ago that the tyranny of Nazis, Stalinists or Maoists brought us perilously close to a return to dark ages.

We crossed the wide cobbled area in the warm sunshine and settled at a table with the right combination of shade and warmth for total comfort. A smiling waiter arrived whose life appeared not to be solitary, poor, nasty or brutish. If he didn`t lose some weight it threatened however to be quite short. He took our coffee order and then, with a mischievous smile, pointed to the sumptuous array of exquisite pastries which had just emerged from somewhere. As if we didn`t already know it he made us aware that temptation has not departed from our sunnier world. It has simply changed its form. We succumbed but felt that there were no doubt more sinful ways of passing the morning.

As with the other parts of Italy I have visited I left with no sense that I had come close to knowing Bologna. It was a cursory first visit and my impressions were, of necessity, partial, but they were almost entirely favourable. For a city which has so many great buildings devoted to the afterlife and such packed congregations in these churches and cathedrals it offered many pleasures to those who love the more earthly pleasures of colour, life, food, music, history and genial companionship.

Acknowledgements

I should like to thank Kris Krug for his invaluable help with the fraught business of creating pdf files and to his wife, the novelist, Pamela Warren, for useful and perceptive suggestions. Tolstoy never had to wrestle with the challenges of jpeg, pdf, png files or multiple editions of Windows and Word. If he had he might have turned out even more strange than he did. I am very grateful for these wise guides through the modern labyrinth.